Think Fearlessly to Grow Wealthy

A seven-stage Health Blueprint to navigate you away from fear and towards action, turning life's obstacles into opportunities for growth.

By

Julia Leckey

Table of Contents

PRAISE FOR *Think Fearlessly to Grow W(H)ealthy*

"A transformational read that makes you dream bigger and get braver"

Charlie Brooks (actress and entrepreneur)

For my boys Fred, Max and Eddy who are the meaning of my life.

For my parents who are the foundation of my life.

For Christina who helped bring this book to life.

In memory of Jacqueline Gold OBE, one of life's most inspirational women whose's endless support and encourgament spurred me on when my dreams just felt like dreams and needed to become real.

The Fearless Mindset Mission

Reshape your habitat.

Stop the guilt.

Unlock the shackles.

Ignite a fire.

Define a new purpose.

Create a new story.

Inspire change.

Build your values.

Live daily your goals.

Break the rules.

Start a movement.

Hunt for new opportunities.

Find the calmness within.

Pause to reflect.

Act as though it is impossible to fail.

Begin each day anew.

The more you take time to choose your thoughts and understand your true nature, the better you can drive change.

About The Author

"Julia has this amazing gift of hope that she gives to people. It's like a shining light of magical words that empowers people to heal from within. I'm not sure you even realise how powerful it is. You are an inspiration!"
—Jacqueline Gold CBE Chief Executive of Gold Group International and Ann Summers.

When Julia hits a crossroads in her own life, she climbs one of the highest green hills near her parents' home in Shrewsbury and looks across the beautiful Shropshire countryside. At the top of her voice, she shouts out how she feels and what she needs, in the certain knowledge that no one else can hear. As she climbs back down that hill's well-worn path, she understands that the universe has listened and is already weaving its web to help. Clarity lights the way forward. It is this boundless creativity, enthusiasm and passion for life that Julia channels to inspire and light the way for thousands of people on similar journeys to yours.

As a Henley Business School and ICF-accredited Executive Coach, Julia is an intuitive, empathetic listener with incredible energy. In her career, Julia Leckey has helped many well-known global brands to lead, succeed and grow their businesses. She has also set up, scaled, and sold two of her own successful companies. Now, having beaten two aggressive cancers and learned to live with the fear of death, Julia is using her experience and expertise to help people become more powerful in the face of *their* fears. Empowering and inspiring, *Think Fearlessly to Grow W(H)ealthy* is filled with stories, ideas, and actions for unlocking your natural power and transforming your future life today.

Authors Socials:

www.julialeckey.com

Linkedin: JuliaLeckey

Instagram: @julialeckeyauthor

Twitter: @JuliaLeckey1

Facebook.com/JuliaLeckey

Authors Coaching website: www.thinkingfearless.com

Why This Book?

"Life's path can be fearful, unpredictable, and joyful in equal measure, so let the adventure begin"
—Julia Leckey

I wrote this book because I've had problems in my own life and have seen similar problems in other people's. Regardless of age, money, status, race we all experience challenges in our lives. I've had those days where it was incredibly hard to get out of bed, to motivate myself to move forward and begin the day anew. At times that fear was devastating. Fear of the future, setting up a new business (and I've set up two), fear of death and dying (I've had two cancers), fear around having children (I've had two of those as well), fear about relationships (I won't say), life, money, fear about fear, and fear about experiencing more fear! It's overwhelming, it's paralysing but I really want to reassure you that when I have allowed myself to really feel and listen to that fear, instead of just pushing it down or running away, I have been able to move through it and beyond!

Why me? Because I sense, from my heart and soul, an obligation to myself, my community, and my family, a responsibility to achieve my potential in this short life. To shine as brilliantly as I can for as long as I can and hope that my passion gives you the courage to shine. Because by kindling our personal passion and light, it can aid others and our society, which so desperately craves that profoundly feminine light and energy that we all have to offer.

On my coaching journey, fear is the biggest topic that comes up from my leadership clients. People find themselves in difficult situations, in places of fear, not knowing what to do, really wondering about the meaning of their life. Where are they heading? What are their goals and ambitions? What is their place in the world? What is next? Fear can really limit your thinking.

I hope that by reading *Think Fearlessly to Grow W(H)ealthy,* you will unleash your natural, inner power to achieve extraordinary results. This book will act as a guide for you to examine your life, take the time to get to know more deeply your inner self and your unique gifts, develop your inner purpose and a growth mindset through stories, exercises, and techniques to help you build an inner powerhouse.

MY STORY

I used to think that with enough willpower and hard work I could do anything.

But there is nothing like growing two seven-figure business, getting cancer twice, giving birth to a 1lb baby three months prematurely and a husband having a heart attack at 52 to make you realise there are things in life you simply cannot control.

What I learned through this time was that life is like the waves of the ocean, always changing. Such unexpected surprises and shocking problems can also make you realise that everything is impermanent. Everything changes eventually, so bad situations also change for the better with time.

A few years ago, I ran into the sea, determined, eager and filled with life. I badly timed my entry into the waves and, before I knew it, I was dragged under the water. Every time I tried to get up, another wave would wash over me and pull my head under. Within minutes I couldn't breathe, think, or break the surface. Thankfully, a friend grabbed the back of my swimsuit and pulled me out. When I remember dark moments in my life, this is what it feels like – those waves just pouring over my head relentlessly with no respite or time to take a breath. But with such dangers or overwhelming problems comes a new awareness and, when I embraced the unfolding experience with mindful awareness, I realised that I didn't need to change to be a radically better or stronger person. I only needed to roll along with the changes, accept them, pivot and try to make my comeback stronger than my setback.

I came to realise that life is filled with problems and unexpected surprises and sudden changes like those powerful waves in the ocean BUT these changes allow you to see new opportunities, new doors opening and new thoughts. Life is not fixed at one steady pace with no room for possibilities or creativity. It's filled with change, energy, and pace and sometimes the hardest pivots you make bring with them the greatest possibilities. What is important in those moments that the big waves hit is how your thoughts and mind embrace and roll with them.

With new experiences came a new spiritual awareness. Know that life is full of changes, some unexpected and scary. Know also that you can ride the energy of those changes and arrive somewhere fresh and rewarding. You use your gifts and sing your unique song!

In those moments, I always ask myself:

Is the change within my power to resist?
What's the worst that can happen if I make a change?
What is the consequence of not making changes?
How can I grow without change?
How can I use this opportunity to move towards a better place?

Childhood – A Growth Mindset

My mom and dad were Salvation Army ministers, spending hours in dozens of soup kitchens helping the homeless, counselling scared and lonely people and being good human beings. It was something they loved doing and it brought them great satisfaction but it involved moving from place to place and never having time to put down roots. My sister and I were just children and, after eight years of living in damp Salvation Army houses on a very low income, our parents had enough of feeling tired and overwhelmed with responsibility and not being able to give us the family home they dreamed of. They stopped hanging onto what wasn't working any more, gathered up their girls, took stock of their skills and experiences, then made their next radical change. After living with my dad's parents for four months and my mom's sister for six, they saved up enough money for a deposit to buy a two-up, two-down house squeezed in the middle of a terrace. In this modest first home they had both stability to nurture their family, and time in abundance to help anyone and everyone in the local community. Dad retrained to be a teacher and Mom a social worker.

When my sister turned 13 and I was 12, my dad realised that there was very little for kids our age to do in the local area. So, he set up a youth club in the local Salvation Army hall. He got a small government grant, enough to buy a basketball net, a pool table and a table-tennis table (he still plays every Monday night at 75 years young). He was also able to buy stock for a tuck shop and kicked off the club every Friday night. In just four weeks, we went from the three of us (me, Dad and my sister) to 80 kids! Even the tough, cool kids came in out of the cold to hang out in our warm little Salvation Army haven.

My parents have the principles of this book ingrained into their DNA and they passed on their loving, hard-working values to us. They tackled every situation from a place of hope and love, not fear of what would go wrong or the fear of making mistakes. They believe in learning and growing in life, the power of joyful moments, being surrounded by the right tribe and helping the less fortunate. They live life light-heartedly but diligently. They have always seen the connectedness of all things and the need to live as one with each other. Indeed, they have often been the glue that binds the community together.

Coming Unstuck

By 39, I co-owned a very successful branding business, was married to a loving husband, had two beautiful kids and a phonebook full of friends. I tried to be everything to everyone, often waking in the middle of the night, heart flying, mind racing and plates spinning, propelling me through the universe at full throttle. It was how I thought you had to be if you wanted success and to squeeze the most out of life. It was how I lived… until one day I suddenly couldn't.

Seven words finally stopped me in my tracks: "I am sorry Julia, you have cancer." As the death sentence echoed around my brain, I started to hear a quiet roar that had been slowly building inside of me that I had been trying to suppress. I had been behaving like a machine. I had been just too busy to stop, plan and think about what fuelled my soul. I'd told myself I didn't have any time to be ill. I'd dismissed my body's attempts to tell me there was something wrong. I'd ignored the pain in my breast for months. Incredibly, part of me wasn't the least bit frightened by the consultant's words. In a way, I felt strangely relieved. It meant that, finally, the huge pressure I had been putting myself under for years would have to stop.

My warp speed turned into slow motion. Like many women I had become a vital cog trying to make so much happen in so many other people's lives but often not prioritising the stuff that made me or those I loved happy. I knew I needed change but I didn't know where to start. My soul was as dry as a knot of tumble weed rolling across a desert.

Driving home having listened to a stage 3 breast cancer diagnosis (that I later discovered had a 75% chance of killing me within five years) the one thought I couldn't get out of my head was, "I have got so much of my life wrong." I looked back and realised I could not remember years of my life. The balance had gone, I hadn't grown in a while and my heart, mind and soul had become numb with overwork and stress. I had been dragging myself out of bed every day for the business I'd been running for so long it had ceased to be interesting anymore. The work no longer fuelled my joy or stimulated my curiosity. What's more, the relationship with my business partner had gone toxic. We'd over-leveraged our personal and business investments, weighed ourselves down with responsibility and lost our valuable friendship in the muddle. For me personally, I'd become weighed down with responsibility but felt there was no personal or spiritual growth. During this whole time, I felt trapped, my fear was so high I sometimes struggled to breathe but, when the cancer was diagnosed, all this stopped.

In my mind, I was going to die. So, unless business meetings were absolutely necessary or urgent, I simply didn't have them. I wasn't going to be part of any new company – I was on a one-way street out of there! The cruel reality had hit me that only the month before I was too busy working to attend fancy events but, that day, I had nothing to do but think of but my life ending. It was as though I'd become trapped behind an expansive glass window, watching helplessly as everyone got on with their lives while I was busy dying. I had found out this fatal truth before I had truly lived. I was envious of the people rushing about around me who had not yet realised that wealth and making wealth would be so unimportant to them on the day that they died.

I felt that sharp energy of anxiety, anger and fear. I also felt the oppressive weight of hopelessness, but I didn't accept it. Every time I breathed, I could feel the energy of those negative emotions, but I redirected it and breathed it in as fuel. I've always been driven and ready to take on challenges, so those fears and challenges became transformed into motivating factors.

As someone who is used to making effective business plans, I knew my priority was getting well from this illness and getting UNSTUCK to fix key areas of my life. This takes a lot of inner confidence, a lot of self-awareness, energy and a willingness to grow.

That I needed a different way of thinking and living became very clear to me. Fear had been running wild for too long – fear of failure, fear of dying, fear of change – but as scared as I was of the cancer, I was equally terrified of going back to living my old life. I was stuck, numb and didn't know what to do. I was staring, wide-eyed, into the Great Unknown.

INTRODUCTION

Curiosity Doesn't Kill Cats

"Whether we are aware of it or not, we will refine the quality of our humanity throughout the course of our lives. More and more, people seek spiritual techniques to help them do this. But joy and suffering will do this for you, too. Every lifetime offers countless opportunities to become more whole."
—Rachel Naomi Remen, My Grandfather's Blessings: Stories of Strength, Refuge, and Belonging

It started with a spark of curiosity for a new way of being and a desire to return to my growth mindset and plan. Not by getting more answers but by asking myself more questions. Yes, there was lots I couldn't control and had a right to be fearful of (I could accept that fact) but there was also so much that I could change, that would make my life better. I just had to discover how to put the work in while undergoing chemotherapy.

I'm not a medical expert—I am writing this book from the heart, sharing the insights I have learned the hard way over the past 10 years—but there is nothing like a good dose of chemotherapy to make you realise that you're not invincible and that life won't last forever. Up to this point I'd felt immortal, and yet deeply lacking in soul. The contentment my parents had, which was part of my DNA, wasn't being fed or watered. The soul searching began – the thinking, the deep inner-work, the meditating, the reading and fasting. Wisdom, gratitude and a deeper appreciation of life came through like green new life, filled with new possibilities. This wasn't an event, a destination or a barrier to break through, it was a new way of living (which I'm still living), with a sense of awareness and connectedness for one's whole sense, connecting more to my feelings, spirit, heart and body and not being passive or afraid of change if something does not feel right intuitively. The secret I found deep within myself is that in order to live well, you must always GROW to feel alive! Reclaim your life power. It's a choice you can take with every breath. It can turn fear into action, trauma into triumph. When you are learning and growing, everything brightens. It makes you feel real, alive, useful, empowered and curious.

So, I started talking to new people, exploring new ways and looking for new opportunities. I was open to trying different things and allowed myself to be vulnerable about sharing my story. I came to see the bigger picture, re-imagining phases in my life as chapters in my life's book. From that point of realisation, whenever I'm not learning and growing, I know that I need to end that chapter of my book and make a change.

If you find yourself avoiding things, distracting yourself or disconnecting from life, then you are not learning and growing – you are stuck and need to put the inner work into moving forward by digging deep into what you want. But don't feel that you must live your whole life as one big, continuous saga. See it in sections, with each chapter adding valuable insight and growth.

In *The 100 Year Life Book* Lynda Gratton speaks about how life used to be viewed in three phases: education, work and retirement. Now, more and more, life has many overlapping and repeating phases: education, travelling, entrepreneurship, PAYE employment, taking a sabbatical, writing a book, starting a family, retraining, career switching etc. Don't wait to retire until you do all those things you always wanted to. Have a 'Plan A' career and a 'Plan B' career running in parallel. Pursue profits and passion with the same energy.

Our Own Universe Within the Ecosystem

As the philosopher and poet Goethe wrote, *"Grey are all your theories, dear friend, but forever green is the golden tree of life. Just trust yourself and you'll learn the art of living."*

– Goethe, Faust: Part 1

No human is ever born alike. The probability of you existing as you is 1 in 400 trillion, which is astonishing – you have already won the lottery of life ahead of trillions of other different players. Along with every other human being alive, you are an extremely lucky person.

Each of us is born into our own distinct universe,one filled with a spectrum of emotions and experiences- fear, growth, joy, sadness, hope, pride, regret, love, hate, and more. It's a universe that spiritual leaders and writers have often portrayed as part of the human ecosystem. Even among our closest friends , there are aspects of their lives that reamin hidden, their unique worlds sometimes veiled from view, and other times, openly displayed to the world.

You were born into this universe to sing your unique song and it's your job to make sure you bloom into full colour. Put your energy into making sure your mini universal garden is so empowered that your mind, body and soul bloom as much as possible.

So, look for what makes you live your authentic life, what makes you glad to get up in the morning, looking forward to spending the day where you can do good for yourself and the world. How do you find this? Not by getting answers but by asking more questions and exploring the inner you. You are a valued human being, and your dream is worth hearing about, so work towards it with concrete steps, even if at first, they are simply baby ones.

This book is a tool for you to use to explore questions about yourself. Like other concepts, it will enable you to see and grasp what otherwise you might miss, it will help you see more possibilities than existed before. Generalisations about humans are not helpful, everyone is unique and therefore this needs to be personalised to you. In a coaching context, I would work with you to create a personal blueprint, but with the help of this book you can adapt my universal blueprint and make it your own.

The seven-stage process of this book includes several vital steps that embrace your inner universe and ecosystem: understanding your fears and putting them into perspective; practising radical honesty and self-love to move out of the fear zone into the essential learning/growing zone; finding your joy and your tribe; becoming more (en)lightened and moving into oneness – into harmony with your tribe and the force that gives origin to everything in the entire universe.

This vital guidance will help you to move from analysis-paralysis into action, from fear into creative flow. You will find more meaning and fulfilment in your life...and much more!

Within this book we also delve into the inspiring journeys of four remarkable and fearless women: Jacqueline Gold, Antonia Belcher, Anna Hemmings and Leanne Pero. These extraordinary individuals have been honoured with prestigious awards as a testament to their unparalleled contributions and unwavering dedication to serving society. Each of their stories is a testament to resilience and determination. Facing life's adversities head-on, they transformed challenges into opportunities, utilising their experiences as powerful platforms for personal and societal growth. Jacqueline, with her pioneering spirit, Anna, exemplifying perseverance, Leanne, demonstrating unyielding commitment, and Antonia, embodying strength in diversity.

Through their outstanding achievements, these women have not only earned distinguished accolades but have also left an indelible mark on their communities. Their journeys serve as a testament to the potential that lies within us all, showing that even in the face of adversity, one can rise above, achieve greatness, and make a lasting positive impact on the world around them.

Challenge Yourself – What Makes You Tick?

As Bonnie Ware asks in *The Top Five Regrets of the Dying,* "What would your biggest regret be if this was the last day of your life?" Among the top answers was "I wish I hadn't worked so hard." For me it is all about defining what 'work' is and what makes me tick. If it lights me up, helps me to learn and grow, then that's not what I consider 'work' – that's living.

Starting up and growing businesses has been a large part of what I do. I have spent my career looking at companies and helping them identify what really makes them tick, what makes them unique and ultimately to improve by bringing out and building on their strengths. I visualise how they could communicate what is important to them and special about them. I ask what they value. This affects how they go forward, how they talk about themselves and influences how their customers and clients relate to them. It involves defining their boundaries – what are they and what are they not? One of the first things I tell my clients is, "Stand for something or fall for anything!"

For years I had been reassuring businesses that "you cannot be everything to everyone," yet as an individual that is exactly what I had tried to be. Ironically, I had never once used my consulting or coaching skills to look at me. I suddenly asked myself: "Why haven't I? I need it too!" I discovered that a lot of what I was doing may have looked great on paper, but it was about somebody else's life. My wise, 70-year-old advisor once said years ago, "It doesn't matter what you achieve, how good you get; if you never believe it, you're always fearful of falling off the edge of a cliff."

I knew that I must stop searching for some kind of perfection – I just wanted to be whole again. So, I asked some close friends what they thought my purpose was. They came back with words like "inspiring", "focused", "driven", "you have millions of ideas", "proactive" and "maybe you should write a book as you've overcome so much". This boost of confidence from people I trusted helped me to move forward at a time when I was feeling vulnerable and stuck. Try it yourself, it's worth a go!

I know that I am still learning and growing. I've worked hard on managing my anxieties and fears because I have found that fear holds us back – even sometimes when you think it is protecting you. It shatters your dreams and makes you wake in the middle of the night in deep sweats. For me, living in fear feels worse than death so I won't allow it to ruin my life.

For many of you reading this, the COVID-19 pandemic was a major wake-up call. The world suddenly halted and people had to rearrange their lives around travel bans, quarantines, curfews and limited social contact. Or maybe it was the financial rug being pulled out from underneath you, forcing you to find another way to earn a living.

Back in 2008, global financial markets collapsed as sub-prime debt futures plunged in value when debts and loans could not be repaid. The US Government and Federal Reserve are thought to have injected approximately $USD 2 trillion to help stabilise the American banking system. This was by no means an isolated intervention by a government to rescue its country's investment banking sector. All around the world, economies were transformed overnight. Catastrophe is often the driving force behind sudden or major changes in career or life in general, but sometimes when life trips us up, we can choose where we land.

Everyone is different but my advice is find what makes you feel good and lights you up, or ask yourself this question, "What makes me tick?" and seek help along the way. The only sure thing in life is change – so how you navigate through this change is what will unleash your power.

You're Only Human

You are not alone in your feelings of anxiety. We all have a million thoughts a day, but which thoughts turn into fear and which thoughts help you to grow wealthy? When I use the word "wealthy" I don't just mean well off for money, but also abundant in physical and mental health, joy and fulfilment, time and freedom, and the richness of strong relationships. If your thoughts today are around fearful things, then in 30 days' time those thoughts will still be fearful unless you make a change. With the help of this book, you can put your fears back into perspective and start creating your vision of tomorrow today.

One rainy day I cracked open my heart and asked the higher powers that be if I could be more of service. Many of us have a god or gods, guardians, muses, spirit guides, angels, gurus or mentors that help us through life. They comfort us in the difficult times and show us the way when we feel lost. I may be the author of the words in this book but I truly believe they have originated from the divine force of energy that flows within us, giving us the spark of life, guidance, and inspiration when we are lost.

We are in a time of great change. Change can be scary, change is restless, comes in waves of highs and lows, but change is also an essential fact of life. If you're going through a great change right now and finding it difficult, I feel for you. I know from my own experience that sudden change can make you feel like you have no control. Our lives are often carefully cultivated to be safe and secure for us and our dependents. When change comes, it can disrupt the security of your finances and bring uncertainty about the future. We are also bombarded by anxiety-inducing events in the media – negative stories on the news, mortgage and energy bills rising, storms and climate change, global pandemics, and lockdowns. It is overwhelming, fearful, and unsettling.

What makes change different today is we are in an ever-accelerating phase of human technological complexity and population growth. Unless we start to think about what we are doing to our planet, none of us will grow truly wealthy. Some will amass huge monetary fortunes, yes, but at the expense of depleting the common wealth of the Earth's resources. This is a huge responsibility for us and our generation. We can kick and scream and say it wasn't our fault, or we can take the responsibility to change what we do have control over and do our part today. You do have control. You can choose which of your thoughts to turn into actions.

10 Good Reasons to Write Things Down

Vividly describing your thoughts and goals in written form is strongly associated with goal success, and people who very vividly describe or picture their goals are anywhere from 1.2 to 1.4 times more likely to successfully accomplish their goals than people who don't. That's a pretty big difference in goal achievement. When I meet young entrepreneurs and ask them about their business models and plans for the future, I am always amazed that 1 in 10 haven't got any plan, values, goals, mission or any form of idea written down.

Here are 10 good reasons to write things down and how they can help:

1. **It clears your mind for higher-level thinking.** It's all about focus and where you place your attention. Where intention goes the energy flows. While you fill in these pages you should try to find a calm and quiet moment to think about yourself and fill it in honestly.

2. **It helps you to focus your emotions and to self-soothe them**. This is about focusing on you to work through inner fears and conflicts and process those emotions. Go to the park, sit on a comfortable bench or maybe lay down in a field, take a

pen and this book with you. Breathe in the air, take off your socks and wiggle your toes in the grass.

3. **It gives you a record of the past that you can refer to**. I've got a terrible memory so at times when I look back at old plans I wrote a few years ago, I'm amazed at how much they have become reality.

4. **It gives you a sense of achievement.** Fill in the dates to give yourself a visual record of the days you've been working on this, so you can look back and reflect on your progress in 1/3/5 years. It gives you a sense of achievement and productivity.

5. **Don't be afraid of going into detail.** Why do you feel this way? This will be something to look back on, reflect on and something to hold yourself to account.

6. **Pause at key points and visit the ice cream van**. Life is made just a little bit easier by enjoying the small pleasures.

7. **Absorb and learn to get helpful insight from the activity.** When you're doing these exercises really feel your inner thoughts, your soul calling and your inner, instinctive nature.

8. **Don't forget to think BIG.** Let your emotions signpost the way. Watch your thoughts and emotions come and go with curiosity. Your soul and inner light will call you and dream the art of the possible. Your heart and mind together will figure out the route.

9. **It makes you more committed to the outcome.** Reflect as you go back over your notes from these exercises. Then, take some time to remember your day, reflect on your week, review your goals over a month and a year. If you write your goals down and keep them in mind, then you're going to be determined to do them.

10. **When you dream at night, notice what your body is trying to say to your mind in these dreams.** When you wake up, write these observations and messages into this book. Let your body have a voice too.

Some Questions to Ask Yourself

Please grab a pen and paper and reflect on a few questions…

1. Write one sentence to describe yourself (write what is right about you, not what you dislike).
2. Ask five friends to describe what is amazing about you in five words.
3. Describe what brings you joy and drives your natural inner power.
4. Was there any time in your life that you have felt out of sync and trapped in fear? Why did you feel that way?
5. What are your natural gifts and how do you use them to power your life and energy?
6. Did you set yourself a purpose/goal(s) for what you wanted to achieve?
7. What is the most amazing thing/moment that you have had/done in life and what results did you achieve? Did you listen to your inner voice and driving force? How did the universe support you in this quest (do you feel like it did)?
8. If you could have the gift of a year doing anything you wanted, what would it be?
9. What is it going to take for you to thrive in the future?
10. If you roll forward 5 years what would you like your life to look like? What changes would you have made to be exactly where you want/need to be?

The Time to Change Is NOW

"Life is like the seasons. We each go through different times and can improve them with skill but cannot change the fact that the times will change."
—Jim Rohn, US entrepreneur

The pandemic brought misery, fear, and isolation to every corner of the Earth. We are left unsure about the future and what that will mean to our way of life, our families, our work.

More than half of 18- to 25-year-olds in the workforce are considering quitting their job. And they're not the only ones. Based on surveys by Microsoft with over 30,000 workers in 31 countries, a 2021 report *The Next Great Disruption Is Hybrid Work – Are We Ready?*, found that as well as 54% of Generation Z workers, 41% of the entire global workforce could be considering handing in their resignation.

Similarly, a UK and Ireland survey found that 38% of employees were planning to leave their jobs in the next six months to a year, while a US survey reported that 42% of employees would quit if their company didn't offer remote working options long term.

When 40% of the global workforce is changing jobs, it is obvious that nothing will be the same. However, this does not mean that it's going to be worse. Crises have always provided an opportunity to rethink how we live, a chance for reinvention and transformation. Knowing our goals and what we stand for is empowering ourselves to navigate the storm. With good judgement and a little luck, it is possible to emerge better off.

I've helped build many brands, and worked with many leaders of companies, and one thing I've learned is the phenomenal power of developing our inner selves, our own goals and vision to make sure we focus, balance, and grow rich in mind, body and soul.

We can all start to take charge of our lives if we want. We can write a new chapter of our life book. We can set a new course so that we learn, develop and arrive at our destination stronger and with better prospects. Feeling fearful and dissatisfied in life isn't about being ungrateful or unhappy; it's about wanting better for yourself and empowering yourself to learn and grow. I want to help you move from the weakest to strongest parts of who you are, from suffering to peace of mind, unleashing your power to flourish. Redirecting and reimagining your own thinking today can magically reshape your life tomorrow!

The time to make the change is now. Why? Humans are needed on this planet; we are part of the evolutionary process that the intelligence of the planet developed to be here right now in this time. We are here and meant to be here. You can question many things about our existence and behaviour on this planet. The human population on Earth reached a staggering 8 billion by the end of 2022, but we have caused or allowed the extinction of millions of living species. So many of us have lost their innate connection with nature and the universal spirit that is here to guide us until, paradoxically, we have become more lost and lonelier on this increasingly crowded planet.

It is vitally important that we remember that there is a universal power that connects and guides us all. You could call it God, Buddha-nature, the Great Spirit and Ancestors, universal consciousness, the Holy Spirit, Mother Nature, Brahman, the Dao, the life force. There are as many names as there are different cultures. The common denominator in every faith is that the highest expression of life urges us to move into love and out of fear, out of the darkness of loneliness, out of insecurity and lack of direction into the love and power of the energy and force that is the essence of this planet. Spirit urges you to think fearlessly, to stand up and be counted as a force of love and energy on this planet.

You might need some help at first to move out of fear-based thinking and into love-based action, and that is okay. We all need a little help at times and, if we are willing to help each other, our home on Earth becomes ever-more connected as one powerful force of love.

Open your heart to the words in this book and walk into a new era of light and love so that we can all be fearless, powerful, and wealthy – in mind, body and soul – and connect more with this planet as ONE. The promise of this book is that it will help you to open up your heart and move into harmonious flow with life and the universe, and in return be held, loved and guided in ways you won't believe.

Promise yourself that you will never give up on this new you. It's a 1000-step journey but getting going takes just one! Momentum will propel you on your journey and it is going to be wilder than your biggest dreams. We can all be knocked off track so don't feel bad if you have hit a rough patch – the answer is about recognising the gaps in your knowledge and knowing what you need to stop doing and start doing in life to make this happen tomorrow.

Get going, live your real life and achieve the extraordinary!

A Powerful Thought: 'What if?'

"You will be as happy as you make up your mind to be right now."
—Benjamin Franklin

Like all projects, this book started with a powerful thought: "What if?" What if…I wrote a book about something that I'm passionate about? Then a belief, a passion and a drive. Thoughts can light up your way or sink you into the deepest, darkest waters.

Thoughts are a powerful force that pull you through life in either a state of paralysing fear or excited anticipation. The thoughts that we pay attention to are the ones that grow in volume and frequency. The future is unknown, so it is for you to choose your thoughts wisely.

According to research using data from MRI brain scans at the Queen's University in Canada, most humans have a new thought every nine seconds. That is around six or seven thoughts per minute, or as many as 6,000 thoughts per day and more than two million thoughts in a single year. The National Science Foundation says it could even be as many as 60,000 thoughts per day for some very bright people! If a person lives for 80 years (or 29,000 days), they could have more than 175 million and up to 2 billion thoughts in their lifetime!

I turned 50 in 2023 and, if I live to be 80, will have 10,950 days left on this wonderful planet Earth. During those remaining days, my many millions of thoughts will influence how happy, fearful, or excited I am, and how much I love, hate, or have apathy towards a situation or person. Thoughts can be your superpower or your archenemy. I can choose to believe that I have 30 years left to make a difference on this planet and act accordingly, or I can give in to fear and wait passively as the sun rises and falls each day. The choice is mine…and yours!

When I visited my friend's ashram in India, I learned that meditation helps free your mind from the bondage of uncontrolled thoughts and can propel you in your path towards true happiness. I have found that to be true. However, this is not a book about sitting quietly in contemplation, but how to think clearly and honestly about your fears and hopes, weaknesses and strengths, so that you can grow in confidence and power to achieve what truly makes your heart sing with joy!

Some Important Facts

"When asked, 85% of UK adults correctly identified symptoms of burnout, which include feeling drained, detached, overwhelmed and having a cynical outlook, procrastination and increased self-doubt."
—Amy Beecham, Stylist Magazine, quoting from the 2020 YouGov study on burnout for Mental Health UK

"In any given week in England, 6 in 100 people will be diagnosed with generalised anxiety disorder (Mind). In the UK, over 8 million people are experiencing an anxiety disorder at any one time (Mental Health UK). Less than 50% of people with generalised anxiety disorder access treatment (Mental Health Foundation)."
—Anxiety Statistics UK/2022 Data/Champion Health

"According to the World Health Organization, 3.6 percent – or about 264 million individuals worldwide – have an anxiety disorder. Additionally, 4.6 percent of females and 2.6 percent of males globally are affected by anxiety."
—The World Health Organization, 26 May 2022

Wealth Starts with Health

Our health is the foundation that we stand upon. All our ambitions, plans, dreams, ideas, lovers, friends, purpose, passion and our life force is contingent on a foundation of good health. Without it we have nothing. And this applies to the health of our environment, also.

Why do humans feel the need to put a price on everything? I read last week that someone had even put a price of $2 million on a single great whale. Over a thousand whales are hunted and killed every year because some people want to make money from selling their meat and body parts.

These graceful creatures who migrate from pole to pole, do more for the quality of our air than all of the trees in the world! Whales absorb carbon dioxide and store the carbon in their bodies, releasing oxygen. Just one great whale will accumulate around 33 tonnes of carbon in its body before it dies and sinks to the bottom of the ocean. Without whales, the levels of carbon dioxide in our atmosphere would dramatically rise. They are an essential part of our ecosystem and should not be killed to make lifestyle products.

At some point our children and grandchildren will wonder, "What on earth were our parents thinking? Why didn't they realise the consequence of their actions and make the changes that were needed so urgently at the time?" Given what we know now, we could make a real difference. Without our health and our planet's health, there is no real collective wealth.

By the end of the 21st Century, when my 12-year-old son is in his 70s and 80s, the planet may not be wealthy or healthy. It simply cannot survive our endless assault on its resources.

We need to redefine wealth and understand that it's beyond money and a price label – rather, it's about social meaning, mental and physical health, spirituality and love of oneself and our planet. Health gives us the freedom to use our time as we wish – let's make the most of it, for Earth's sake.

What It Means to Think Fearlessly

Fear is a natural response to real dangers or threats. While it has helped humans survive throughout evolution, fear can interfere with daily life if it is triggered by *false* threats or *imagined* dangers.

Fear can make us want to lay in bed and hide from the real or *imaginary* monsters outside. So just when you feel at your most scared you also can feel very lonely because you have isolated yourself – not a great combination.

Thinking Fearlessly allows you to find the space to grow and live freely throughout the seasons of life. Finding a way to think with *less fear* will help you to live your life with a new freedom and purpose. It doesn't mean you won't feel fear. But fear will become more of a passenger in the car rather than the driver.

Thinking with *less fear* frees up the mind to expand, allowing you to feel more, to live more, to shine and to feel less alone. You become a cup that has room to be filled with wondrous things. It will create space so that you can move in a new direction. It doesn't mean that life won't still be challenging at times (we all have our sleepy vs energetic days) but when you are living with less fear, it's much easier to find your path and weather the rains and storms that will come your way.

Remember, as human beings we are remarkable and we can achieve extraordinary things. Human beings can turn weeds into gardens, imagination into landscapes, ideas into businesses, baking cakes for fun into scrumptious cake shops. Reach inside yourself and become remarkable. Reconnect with your own natural energy; be more instinctive and achieve remarkable things.

Living with less fear creates a space in your mind to explore where you can "full fill" your true potential. A quest to find your inner self and your own uniqueness, develop your purpose and find your tribe of people who will help you to materialise your dream.

Growing Healthy and Wealthy

We all have a million thoughts a day, but which thoughts turn you into a fearful jelly and which thoughts will help you to grow wealthy? You can choose.

When I was in a poor mental state, I felt deeply unsatisfied even though on paper I had achieved so much. I felt guilty for feeling this way but my soul was longing for more. What more? I kept asking myself.

Then later, even though the cancer was in remission, I doubted the robustness of my health and wealth and so I lived in a perpetual state of fear.

The speed of our contemporary world leaves us less time to think about and plan changes. Adaptation to changes have become automatic and unquestioned. Those four to five hours for daily reflection and observing your life get swallowed up by the time it takes to watch the world via social media. What are you learning from that?

Just like a seed needs soil, sunlight, and water, I needed to reflect in order to work out how to grow. I had to dig deeper into the subconscious to find answers. So, I switched off the TV and, over time, I deeply examined and journalled my life. Why? Because I knew I would drown in my fear if I didn't. This became about survival. On my journey, I came across a

Socrates quote, "The unexamined life is not worth living." If we don't think then we are no more than the animals, he believed, simply eating, sleeping, working, and procreating.

When I examined my life, soul, and heart I found a remarkable answer. I had stopped growing. The opposite of being dissatisfied isn't to be satisfied. The opposite of being dissatisfied is to learn and grow.

The Wealth Health Blueprint

"Being brave isn't the absence of fear. Being brave is having that fear but finding a way through it.'

— *Bear Grylls, TV explorer and author*

When we try to find a way out of a difficult situation, or when we make something entirely new, we are learning and growing the whole time. The fear and anxiety will suddenly turn into excitement and enthusiasm when we realise, "Yes, this is possible!"

It's about how do you turn a problem into a gift and opportunity for growth. You can either be stuck in fear or find a way to move beyond and away from it – it's hard at the time, but if you see every issue like this it helps!

Do you believe in the transformational power of creativity and an ability to change? How confident do you feel to go through a journey to find your potential and then share it with those around you? Don't worry if your confidence is a little lacking at this stage – you will find that confidence as soon as you start to follow your JOY...

Follow these seven steps out of fear into the creative flow of ONENESS.

Facing FEAR – allow yourself to become aware of your feelings, acknowledge them and then move beyond fear
Feeling LOVE and compassion for yourself and for others
LEARNing and GROWing on your way
Experiencing JOY – find it, feel it, use it and shine!
Finding your TRIBE – who to lean into or away from
(EN)LIGHTEN yourself – lighten your load, know where you're heading
ONENESS – experience the joy and creative flow of living with oneness, within you, with your ecosystem, your TRIBE, your home (our Earth)

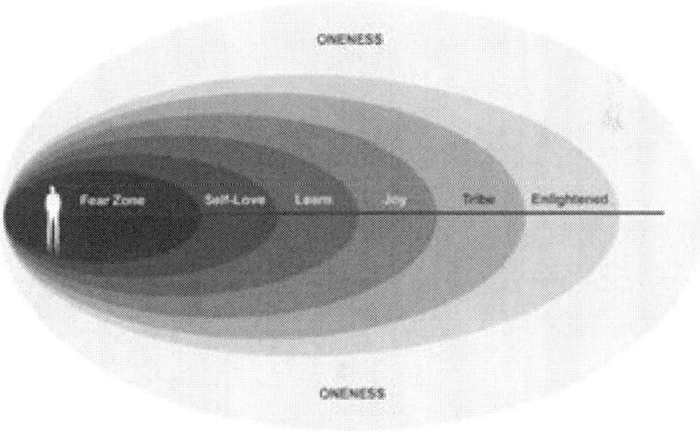

STEP 1: Facing Fear (Escaping the Fear Zone)

"Nothing in life is to be feared, it is only to be understood. Now is the time to understand more, so that we may fear less."

—Marie Curie, Nobel Prize Winner for Physics (1903) & Chemistry (1911)

Many of us become stuck in a mental maze of ideas, anxieties and blockages that I call the "Fear Zone". When we subconsciously give up our power to those fears, they can spiral into self-sabotaging behaviours. Please believe in your own power and agency. You can move your fear out of the driving seat and take back control! Don't make things a problem. Instead, look to understand why and turn your feelings of frustration into fascination.

There are life situations when fear becomes so real it's like a petrifying monster in the room. It is important to breathe and get some perspective. There are simple realities of life, the things we can't change or escape, such as facing mortality, disease and health scares, the seasons, bad weather, job loss, rising costs, parental responsibilities, and so on.

Sometimes fear is so sneaky you don't even realise you are in its clutches. How do you recognise yourself when your mind is swimming in that place of fear?

Fear is often an emotional veil hiding a deeper desire. To penetrate that fear you need to understand what triggers it. Feelings like pride, jealous, anger, aggression, ignorance and desire all hold us back. People have all these emotions but a stronger flavour towards one emotion. What is your fear triggered by? Through awareness and meditation, we create a still mind and we can see what is driving this fear. This moves you from fear to fearing less.

Every day we have a million thoughts, memories, and feelings that distract us from what is real but, if you stop and look, we are here and now in this present moment. You can learn to control your thoughts if you recognise that they belong to the past that has gone or to an imagined tomorrow that is yet to come. They are not real. They are only memories or imagination and they can only control us if we let them.

Fear is just thought, when you think ahead and imagine the worst life ever, that your future is bleak and dark, or full of obstacles and challenges that you can't face. Just remember that it is only imaginary – what you fear has not happened, it's not real.

If you choose your thoughts carefully, trust your intuition and guidance, then your tomorrow will be different than today and your next year will be absolutely unbelievable – the places you'll end up will surprise you! If I had let fear be my driver then I would never have got out of bed, set up two business, lived through my cancers and pivoted to new opportunities that far outweighed the fearful times I thought I was having.

If you start by trying to change the things outside of yourself then you will quickly become frustrated. Do not waste your energy! To fear less, realise that you need to understand yourself and change the inner YOU; understand your fears, your attitudes or judgements, your words and language, your skills, your priorities and goals. How you choose to spend your time will affect your readiness to move forwards.

So, let's start by reflecting and understanding your fears today. Consider them, breathe into them and acknowledge them. What's trapping you in life, what are your vulnerabilities, how do you THINK and speak to yourself? In these ways, reflect honestly on what you are doing today so that you can start making a difference tomorrow.

Aim: to help you understand what is driving your fears. What emotions are you veiling/covering up and what is trapping you and stopping you from moving into the life you desire?

STEP 2: The power of LOVE and SELF LOVE

Often there is so much pain in our hearts that we defeat ourselves with doubt, judgment, and self-loathing. Going through this pain and surviving the feelings that come up enriches your inner life. You get to experience the whole universe of emotions. It difficult when you are down and must build yourself back up again. As J.K Rowling famously said, "Rock bottom became the solid foundation on which I rebuilt my life."

This new energy and insight can make you capable of finding a purpose that is authentic and meaningful. When you drown in fear and trauma, the pain is massive. But keeping hold of self-love and letting go of bitterness will lead you to a path of healing and to a new life. Move beyond this and find love for yourself.

It is important to really take a good look at what self-love means. We are taught that vanity and arrogance are bad qualities. Self-love doesn't mean this. It means being honest and realistic about our strengths (not just our weaknesses), being compassionate to ourselves, learning from our mistakes and allowing ourselves to dream big, because that is how we learn and grow. Love operates at a high and powerful frequency that helps us to flow, grow and learn. Look inwards and see the inner you and love that person fiercely! Love is the power that pulls you into the future.

Aim: to be kinder to the inner you, practice good inner talk, connect with whoever you need in your lifeboat to help you (the friends and family to help), and tame your inner critic (I call mine Jill, I will talk about her later). Self-love is empowering so try to embrace it.

STEP 3: LEARN and GROW by tuning into your natural intuition

"Think of the power that's in the universe – moving the Earth, growing the trees – and that's the same power within you, if you'll only have courage and the will to use it!"

— *actor Charlie Chaplin, as Calvero, Limelight (1952)*

Life is always in motion, growing and evolving. Learning and growing helps you to release your inner power and inner guru – the opposite of learning and growing is being unsatisfied so why be happy with this?

How can you learn and grow and create your own seven-step Health Blueprint for learning and growing? Sometimes we just need a map to show us where we need to go to understand what lights us up and really start to believe that there are opportunities for growth out there in the world. The universe is an infinite thing and there is enough for us all.

Learning doesn't stop when we leave school or college. It is a lifelong process. When was the last time you read a book and learnt something new? Watched a documentary? Went on a course and got a new qualification? Learning is something that is a skill we can improve over time, or it is something that our anxieties or complacency can block us from. It is important to lean into our fears, to move out of our comfort zone, to risk stepping into the unknown, so that we can grow and fully realise a richer, happier future.

Learning is also about understanding YOU. Learning to tap into your inner nature, your gifts, psyche, imagination, ideas and feelings is a powerful route to self-empowerment and resilience. Even though you cannot always see these powerful gifts, they are inside of you waiting to be explored. Build a personality board (I'Il show you how later so hold that thought), a variation of a mood board with images of what you want to BE. Focus on creating the lifestyle you want for the inner/outer you, start creating your online/offline personality boards: how you look + feel, think + act, speak + sound.

Aim: to think about what you need externally to help you to learn and grow. To learn more about YOU and your eco-system/inner universe. Define your values, your purpose, how you look, think, and speak in the world. What does your inner (your fire/energy) and outer resources (financial, network) need to look like to support you?

STEP 4: Experience JOY

"In the small matters trust the mind, in the large ones the heart."

—Sigmund Freud

Fundamentally, all creatures seek happiness. Humans desire more than ordinary happiness though. If you are honest, you desire JOY – the feeling of fulfilment and oneness with the world. Joy starts with a sense of curiosity, an ember of excitement that can grow.

I believe joy comes when you are using gifts, the things that light you up, make your laugh, and smile. That can be your direction in life, your passions. These are your torches in the dark. Those are the things that will illuminate in those dark moments and you know when you have found your joy as the hours slip by in the blink of an eye and you feel energy around them. They fill you with such in-depth pleasure and hope. If you have decided that you want change and are ready to live that joy, allow yourself to imagine the art of the possible, let your joyful imagination and creativity run wild. A helpful starting point could be to decide what is your north star. Where do you want to head towards in life? Writing this down will give you something to focus on.

Next, so that you can increase your motivation towards a new direction, try creating visual mood boards of what you want (I'II show you how later so hold that thought). These are collections of images that you can draw, cut out of magazines, download from the internet and assemble around a chosen theme. If you place these in a prominent position on your computer or physical desktop, they become a daily reminder and powerful motivating tool to achieve your heart's desire. By stepping out of the constricted, suffocating feeling of fear, you allow yourself to discover what makes you truly happy and to start experiencing real fulfilment and joy in your work and life. Be brave. What holds you back is not your capabilities, it is fear of failure. So, fear less and move forward!

Aim: to define your gifts and what lights you up and work out how you use these gifts to head towards what you want in life.

STEP 5: Finding your TRIBE

Do you recognise who really helps you, who puts wind in your sails and powers your boat? Look at everyone in your life and take an inventory. It could be your immediate family and relations, the friends that you are closest with, your colleagues at work, your trusted advisors or mentors, a spiritual leader or elder, or even people you communicate with online. This is your time to find your tribe. To focus on your relationships. Family and friends are essential to long-term happiness, and the most important relationship is with your partner. Invest in this relationship every day. Don't keep score – focus instead on forgiveness, generosity and engagement. Cherish the people who can help you turn your dream into reality. This could include the people you rely on day in, day out, but also people you need once in a blue moon for a specific but very important job. It is important when choosing who is in your tribe to understand their strengths and weaknesses and how you can work together.

You will know the friends you should lean into – learn to recognise the people you should move away from. They can either light you up or drain your spirit, they give you energy or exhaust you. Help yourself to thrive, to rejuvenate, to share your truth and be with people who support your growth.

Once you find your tribe radiate out and find your community, your network, and your global social stance in the world. When I have bad times in life, I text five friends and ask them why they are my friend, what they like about me. Their answers always light me up! When I was poorly, I wrote letters to all my close friends thanking them for being my friends. The outpouring of love and tribal affection was so overwhelming during this period that it lit me up like in the *Monsters Inc* movie when the children's laughter powered the city.

Aim: to define who is in your tribe, who lights you up and who is toxic and needs to go.

STEP 6: LIGHTEN YOUR LOAD and ENlighten yourself

"Out of your vulnerabilities will come your strength."

—Sigmund Freud

The six step is about feeling and living a more enlightened or lightened life. To allow yourself to grow into this healing healthy life plan, to nurture yourself till you feel lighter in your mind, body, and soul. To daily continue the journey to discover the powerful inner you and to build your greater inner knowledge. To hold the belief system that allows you to be kinder and lighter with yourself. To act and believe like it's impossible to fail.

Moving forward helps you shake off the past. You won't feel stuck, you will feel liberated that you are moving forward with a fresh view. You have a new strategy to move towards, to navigate past the obstacles. This makes you more creative and lighter. When you have a way forward you find more harmony and are less burdened by fear or the past. You are looking at the world in a new way.

Why did I take my healing journey and plan seriously? Because I wanted to live a new empowered life, clear of burdens and fear and anxiety, to free myself to feel lighter and more colourful and creative. This takes curiosity, courage and creative planning. A need for boundaries to protect a healing and healthy mindset...you need time for change to bed in and grow, to align, to have the time to create the life you want with all your new exciting plans. As a society we need to start shifting our consciousness into a lighter way of being. Good mental and physical health is wealth, lightness, and love. keep your vision, purpose, mission for the future at the front of your mind when you are developing the lifestyle you want to have. You will feel delicate at first but as it gets a habit, your boundaries are protected and you will feel the lightness.

The most meaningful things in life are heavy. And life itself can be more meaningful when it is hard. Those challenges sharpen us, push us, force us to go beyond our self-imposed boundaries and make us create boundaries to protect ourselves. We don't appreciate these teachings while we're in the middle of them. But when we come out the other end, we realise we wouldn't have become better people without them. We wouldn't feel the lightness until that heavy load has been lifted from our backs.

To lighten the load, you need to think deeply about how the next year can be different than the last year. If you want to feel lighter, what can you change? With all your experience, gifts, values and ideas, and your north star in mind, what will the next 1/3/5 years look like for you? Then step into this lighter zone, where the real growth happens, and start living an extraordinary life. Follow your dreams, live life to the full and live that life worth living.

Aim: to create a lighter feeling, have your 1/3/5-year growth goals, plan and aims in place. Your seven-step plan is being activated daily. Your legacy is being created and what you can/cannot control is allowing you to flow more with life. You are taking massive action, being focused, and committing in these times of uncertainty.

STEP 7: Living with the concept of ONENESS

"It's a great human-interest story that we are now able to map the abundance of all of the major elements found in the human body across hundreds of thousands of stars in our Milky Way."

— *Jennifer Johnson, Science Team Chair SDSS-III APOGEE survey and Professor at Ohio State University*

We are each our own person, our own unique universes. We are also humans, mammals, animals, a living organism, a collection of matter here and now and a field of energy interacting with other fields of energy. We are also part of the total cosmos at one with all and everything and with the total universe. We are part of this whole ecosystem a larger universe beyond ourselves. We are unique and separate, but we are also part of a whole, since all things are related. I love the idea that we are made of the things that make up stars, that 97% of the raw materials that constitute our physical bodies were forged in the bellies of distant, long-extinguished stars. It makes complete sense. Carbon, hydrogen, nitrogen, oxygen, phosphorus and sulphur are the crucial building blocks of life and this makes me truly believe we are ONE and meant to be here on this planet. We are all one life force within this universe, each with our own journey and purpose to fulfill.

If we think about our health, we will all become wealthier in mind, body and soul, becoming more empowered. We know that change brings fear and fear does not nourish us or the world. When we make the inward change, it ripples outwards, creating harmony. A new era. Radiate the new you into your community, the people around you, your work colleagues, the people in the street. When your love starts, and joy start to flow outward, you will see a propound growth of your inner light and the effect it has on others.

When we are at one, we don't feel lonely or disconnected we feel part of the whole, part of a tribe and part of the bigger universal picture. We can tap into this feeling of oneness within our sixth sense, the creative imagination of our subconscious, through which ideas, plans, and thoughts flash through our mind – those hunches or inspirations you sometimes ignore. Like all living beings we have infinite intelligence – the power that permeates our atoms and grows acorns into trees, powers the waves to flow across the ocean and for 4 billion years has evolved our planet into one living, breathing world.

On a micro level, we comprise of 10 billion human cells and ten times as many friendly micro-organisms. There are as many micro-organisms in your body as bright stars in the Milky Way.

Life is full of energy and so are you. If we start to think as ONE within ourselves, in our mind, body, and soul, we become ONE. We can then start to become more connected with ourselves and our bodies. We can learn to mediate, scan, and listen to our bodies and understand what it needs. I did a Rieke course that taught me to think as ONE in relation to my cancer diagnosis. I hoped and believed that each one of my cells would be well. I wished them loving energy every day.

When we act more as ONE in our organisations at work, our local community, our country, our planet we all push in the same direction, respecting the same values, and achieving the same goals. Businesses spend millions creating a mantra, to unite their workforce and customers behind one powerful vision. *"Just do it"* says Nike. It empowers its employees and customers to go for it.

When we understand the power of acting as ONE, we can all work to save this planet so we have a future. Remember that the life force within you and your millions of atoms, protons and molecules is the same energy and force that flows throughout the universe.

Now, I want to run through each of the steps in detail to help build a new transformed inner you.

STEP 1: Escaping the FEAR ZONE

"For a long time, it had seemed to me that life was about to begin – real life – but there was always some obstacle in the way, something to be got through first, some unfinished business, time still to be served, a debt to be paid... then life would begin. At last it dawned on me that these obstacles were my life'"

— *Alfred d' Souza*

Many of us become stuck in a mental maze of ideas, anxieties and blockages which, as I said in the introduction, I call the Fear Zone. We all have things that we fear. Your triggers will be different to mine but the feeling of fear can be the same – a sense of closing in, a feeling of paralysis and a lack of hope. When your mind is taken by fear or chronic worry your life can be overtaken by that fear and you cannot live easily in the present moment. Fear is the biggest obstacle in life because it can spiral you into self-sabotaging behaviours.

In this section I'm going to identify some fears that I've had, and also the worries some of my business clients and people that I'm coaching face. A lot of these are the simple realities of life, the things we can't change or escape: facing mortality, disease and health scares, the seasons, bad weather, job loss, rising costs, parental responsibilities, and so on.

The key to recognising when you're in a place of fear is simply by being aware of how it feels in your body and mind. With awareness comes understanding and with understanding you can start helping yourself to move through and forward.

In your own unique universe, what is driving your fear? Fear is a veil that often hides deeper emotions (pride, jealously, anger, aggression, ignorance, and desire). What is triggering the fear emotion in you? Through awareness and meditation, we create a still mind and we can see what emotions are behind this fear. This moves you from fear into understanding more/fearing less.

LIFE is for living and growing, while FEAR is the opposite. It's a sense of dying, shrinking, and giving up. Please don't give up, believe in your own power and ability to move forward. Don't make things a problem, look for a solution, turn your feelings of frustration into fascination.

Some of the things we fear:

*Change
*Sickness
*Conflict
*Death
*Lack of time

*Loneliness
*Rejection
*Failure
*Appearances
*Ageing
*Not having enough money

If you start by trying to change the things outside of your control then you will quickly become frustrated. Don't waste your energy! (I expand on this more later with a helpful exercise). To fear less, realise that you can change YOU: your attitude or unhelpful fears of imagined failure or judgement, your words, how you choose to spend your time, your language, your skills, your priorities and goals. So, let's start by reflecting on the inner YOU today. What do you fear? Be honest about what's happening today to make you so fearful. Which of your fears are based in the reality of the here and now? Understanding that fear can be fuelled by imagination, take a good look at what you are really working with so that you can start making a difference tomorrow!

Why is Fear a Problem in our Society?

I often refer to the book *Why Zebras Don't Get Ulcers* by Robert M. Sapolsky. This book presents research evidence on the (mostly negative) impact of stress on your body functions, from hormonal balance to cardiovascular risk, from growth to reproductive system – everything. Stress and anxiety are experiences like fear, trapping us in despair and lack of hope. It's a sense of hiding, closing the door, not living, closing yourself to growing or learning. We live today in so much fear and anxiety. Anxiety of failure, of death, of life itself, changing jobs, losing our job, exploring beyond our boundaries on and on. Anxiety and fear are around every corner making us lose faith, our ability to move forward or even at times to enjoy the one life we have. Fear outstays its usefulness, paralysing or blocking us long after the actual threat has gone.

Animals have the ability to run, hide and recover from fear with speed. Watch a lion chase a frantic gazelle on a TV programme. If the gazelle manages to escape, it will begin to calmly start grazing again. Always alert but seemingly content. As soon as the danger is over, the gazelle is no longer is a state of fear and flight. We, unlike the gazelles, don't stop running and we often cannot calm down quickly. We have overactive imaginations and cannot always distinguish the real and present dangers from the remembered or feared ones.

When we operate at danger level so often that we get used to the feeling of constant danger, it can leave us paralysed, unable to think clearly, move forward or gain momentum. Anxiety and fear, the most primitive of all emotions, overwhelm us from the inside.

The first time I had a panic attack was just after I turned 40. I'd heard about them from friends but had no idea what it meant to really feel anxiety and fear rippling through every cell of my body. It was paralysing. I felt just like that gazelle seeing a lion approaching from afar, frozen quickly by fear. From that time onwards I sought to learn to liberate myself from this feeling, from this fight or flight mechanism.

FEARLESS THINKING

Ask yourself...

Have you ever felt fear?

Do you know what triggered it?

What deeper emotion was the fear covering?

Stand in front of the mirror and talk the story of your fear until you know and recognise it.

The Lighthouse (fear of death)

I was once told by a friend that I am like a lighthouse. I was born with an inner fire/optimism that burns brightly. They said that when I turn my attention in one direction with intensity, I not only bring awareness and illumination but hope for the future and all its possibilities. It could be a relationship, a project, a search for a new job, anything that I focused on I could bring a new passion or purpose to it.

Then one day I lost my shine, my hope, my optimism, my ability to drive my projects with such intensity. My clarity of purpose disappeared, as if my inner light had been snuffed out. I hoped it was still inside of me but it sure as hell felt gone for a long while.

After a little introspection, I realised what it was – I'd allowed fear deep into my life and with it came an intense feeling of loneliness and a lack of connection and meaning. Fear was like a dense smoke that crept through the door of my lighthouse, up the hundreds of stairs and blocked my light. The fear became so real in my mind that it gathered a shape and form and started following me around. The fear, or Fear Monster, as I came to call it, brought with it not only a blanket of fear that obscured my guiding light but put up new obstacles within me – a lack of drive, energy, or even willingness to grow and learn, a deep fear for myself and insecurity about all that I was and was ever going to be.

I watched with envy a video of myself the year before my light went out. I hardly recognised the person looking back at me. She was bright, energetic and fearless. What had happened to me? I believed that my cancer diagnosis had caused me to consider my mortality, and created a realisation of the reality of death.

One day I was happily going about my normal life and the next day the fear appeared like a monster. It followed me round my home, came to my favourite restaurants, girls' nights out, swimming lessons with my son, on weekends away and holidays abroad. I could feel it creeping up on me in the night. I could smell its breath on my face when walking in the park with my friends. It never left me alone.

On some days, the fear of death made my throat clamp and my breathing laboured. No one could tell me when the Fear Monster would appear next, in fact no one knew it was there as only I could feel it. Some days I would smile at friends but then catch a glimpse of it from the corner of my eye. I used to try and hide from the Monster. But hiding didn't make it go away. It made it worse. The fear grew and grew. I'm sorry to be so vivid but to describe real fear to friends I need to be more literal. I was so scared of cancer it became my Fear Monster for a while.

To make it real I needed to describe it to myself, to acknowledge it existed in my life. I had to face the truth that my world had suddenly got scarier and out of control. I knew I had to change and find a new mindset which was free from fear so I could live in the NOW.

Yes, I needed to plan for the future, but not at the expense of today. So, I wrote a letter to my Fear Monster to see if getting my feelings out could bring about a new perspective and a change of thought process.

Dear Fear,

I am aware of you...but you will no longer scare me; you will no longer wake me up in the night or be able to overshadow me. Your days of being large and scary in my life are over. You created so much fear in me that I became lost in your shadow. No more.

Now, I will look every day at the Sun and you will fall behind me like my shadow. You will not sit in the driving seat of my car but become a passenger who doesn't decide the path I take. So, here's the thing, we need to learn to live together. I've decided to live to be 90 and that's what I'm going to tell myself every day.

From now on I'm going to live in the PRESENT, wake up and say hello to the day, breathe deeply the air, laugh with my children, live my dreams, feel the wind in my face. I'm going to live my life to the full. So, from today I am going to embrace you. Let's learn to live side by side. I'm here. I'm present by your side as your friend.

Love from Julia x

FEARLESS THINKING

What's your biggest fear?

Is your fear driving your life?

Write a letter to your biggest fear today and tell your story.

Next time you feel your own Fear Monster chasing you, think about the following

Truth 1:

Feeling fear is like being stuck deep in a muddy field, unable to move.

Truth 2:

The fear will never go away unless you are aware of it and face into it.

Truth 3:

Pushing through fear is about living in the now. All my fear is around the future that hasn't happened yet.

Truth 4:

Having a plan or a big goal gives you something to aim for – a purpose, a north star – and moves you away from fear. (More on this later).

Truth 5:

We are all going to die. We are all terminal. But having cancer doesn't mean you will die tomorrow or the next day – it's not an instant death sentence, it's a chronic illness that many people survive.

Book recommendations:

Radical Remissions: Surviving Cancer Against All Odds by Kelly A. Turner

Heal Your Body by Louise Hay

Wood from the Tree (fear of my children failing)

There is so much pressure on parents and children today, that the fear of failing at school or in a career choice is enormous. Last year, for example, I was intensely worrying about my 17-year-old son failing his exams. It wasn't based on reality or fact but out of worry. He had always done well academically but I didn't see him sitting at the table doing his homework as often now that he was older and more independent.

I got so worried that I asked a group of friends to help by doing a coaching exercise with me. I gave them each a pen and asked them to listen and respond to me talking on a subject that was worrying me for a couple of minutes.

I asked them to do three things:

1/Draw a picture that comes to mind when I am talking.

2/Write a word to describe how you feel when I am talking.

3/Write a question for me to think about, to explore my feelings and get perspective.

I took my watch out and set my timer for 2 minutes and went for it…

"Ok, I'm worrying about my 17-year-old son. He's lying in bed till 12 attending school only 17 hours a week, spending hours in his room gaming and going to the gym a few times a week. He did do well in his GCSEs without any help from me or his dad and he had a tough time through covid as they were hardly in school for a year. It's just I'm worried that I need to step in and help more or I fear he will fail his A Level exams. He seems to be doing very little. I admit I'm not sure because he's a secretive person. But if he fails, I fear he won't go to uni, he won't do computer science which he loves, and I will blame myself as I haven't helped him. Here I am a coach and when I try to talk to him, he looks at me like I'm bonkers. It's created issues in the house, and I've even started getting fixated with asking him when his homework needs to be handed in and I've never done this ever before. When the school texted me to say his homework was three days late last week, I chased and chased him and he told me to lay off as I didn't know the school system. It makes him grumpy, me concerned and his dad is stepping in to help but I am really starting to fear the worst..."

I paused and waited, they started to scribble busily on their napkins.

Example answers to my questions from a friend:

1/Draw a picture that comes to mind when I am talking.

She drew a STAR with my son's name (meaning he is a star)

2/Write a word to describe how you feel when I am talking.

She wrote SIGH (meaning she wants me to have more faith in my son)

3/Write a question for me to think about, to explore my feelings and get perspective.

She asked, *"Whose fearing failure the most? him or you?"*

The results were so revealing and really helped me to calm down. Try this exercise yourself next time you feel overwhelmed with worry.

FEARLESS THINKING...

Try it.

Talk for 2 minutes on something that you have lots of fear around to yourself or a few friends...give it a go because it's a very powerful way of becoming deeply aware of fear.

Wind in the Sails (fear of being in the wrong job)

There is lots of fear around career change from the people I coach and people I've employed. When is it the right time to move on? What fear is holding you back from making that important decision?

Apple founder Steve Jobs famously said:

"Remembering that I'll be dead soon is the most important tool I've ever encountered to help me make the big choices in life. Almost everything – all external expectations, all pride, all fear of embarrassment or failure – these things just fall away in the face of death, leaving only what is truly important. Remembering that you are going to die is the best way I know to avoid the trap of thinking you have something to lose. You are already naked. There is no reason not to follow your heart. No one wants to die. Even people who want to go to heaven don't want to die to get there. And yet, death is the destination we all share. No one has ever escaped it, and that is how it should be, because death is very likely the single best invention of life. It's life's change agent. It clears out the old to make way for the new."

If today was the last day of your life, would you still want to do what you are doing now? What if the answer is NO? Will you change your job now? What is holding you back?

One of the things people fear most in life is changing job. There are countless reasons for that fear because income is vital for so many aspects of people's lives. When I felt like I was trapped in a job I hated, it was like I was struggling against a head wind that was always pushing me backwards, blocking my advancement. When work feels like such an effort, eventually it becomes unbearable. You have to use all of your energy just to move a foot forward.

If you ever feel you're not growing or learning then watch out! You are in a head wind! It's time to rethink, prepare for Plan B and head for a new future. Watch the signs, get out of there and get moving! Hanging on in there just waiting for the head winds to get stronger, will exhaust you. Gather up all your knowledge, experience, magic, and energy and make a change. JUMP into the unknown!

Maybe it doesn't need to be quite a leap of faith, perhaps it can be more of a planned step from A to B that moves you forward, fully prepared, into a new adventure.

When you are in a job or situation you love, it's like wind in your sails. Wow, this is the most amazing feeling when you're flowing with life. Your sail is up, the wind powers you onwards and it's effortless. You are fearless and moving swiftly through the natural ocean of life. It's what is sometimes called being in a state of flow.

This happens to me when I am writing. I glance at my watch and it's 2pm and then what feels like three seconds later I look again and it's 6pm. This is effortless freedom. The hours race by unnoticed and my heart is on fire. If you can't decide what job to do next and fear change, look out for those times when you have wind in your sails. You'll probably find it is when you are following a passion or using a gift that lights you up and drives you forward.

FEARLESS THINKING...

When do you feel like you're in a headwind?

Have you woken up over the last month/quarter/year and thought NO or YES every Monday morning?

When do you ever feel the wind in your sails? What revs your engine? What gifts were you using when this happened?

Could these clues suggest a clever future move?

The Dangers of Having a Front (fear of being vulnerable)

Being seen as a strong, independent woman and putting on a smiley face comes in useful. You know that face I mean. The one that means you can blend in, stay low, or smile and inspire confidence when deep down you're suffering. When you meet friends in the street, or a colleague at work, and they ask how you are, do you try to hide how you are really feeling and just use the smile?

You can't possibility answer, *"I'm lonely, I'm scared, I'm hurt, I'm fearful, I'm out of my depth"*.

So, you smile and say *"I'm ok"* and everyone moves on with their lives saying to others *"she looks well even though I hear she's not"* and you walk away feeling that little bit more alone just blending in and not standing for anything.

We do it because our culture is built on having a front. On social media, newspapers, glossy magazines, and videos, we learn to project a front to the world. But at times all we all need is a little help. As my wise mom says, *"A little help is worth a lot of pity."*

We are pack animals that need to feel loved, we long for the energy and connection of each other. We were not born to be alone. Covid-19 may have killed many people but there are fears that many more will die from the loneliness of lockdown – that feeling of being isolated in the world.

When my husband had a sudden heart attack at 52, I was stunned. As our world shrank and caved in, the planet kept on spinning. The washing still needed to be done, my business still needed to be run and my sons still needed their dinner.

On the second night when I got home from hospital at 9pm, there was a bag with a pizza, garlic bread and a bottle of wine on my doorstep, with a note from the moms at school saying that they wanted to cook for us every night for a week while we visited the hospital. As I was about to text and say 'How lovely but please don't worry', I stopped and considered just how valuable a little help was. It was like gold dust fluttering through the sky on a snowy day. It was a sign that the universe (the lovely school moms) was helping us, so I gratefully accepted the gesture.

The next time a neighbour or a friend at work asks about you, be honest *("I feel lonely" or "I'd love a little help")*. Vulnerability isn't a weakness or something to fear, so don't camouflage yourself. It's the first step to being connected to a community and feeling more alive. You have no idea how many people's days could be brightened if you catch their eye, smile and say, *"Hi, how are you, are you ok?"*

FEARLESS THINKING…

Think of the things you need a little help with, list the top 3

Who can you ask for help?

How can you help them in return?

Fight, Fight, Fight or Flight
(fear of conflict or confrontation)

"We can't be afraid of change. You may feel very secure in the pond that you are in, but if you never venture out of it, you will never know that there is such thing as an ocean, a sea. Holding onto something that is good for you now, may be the very reason why you don't have something better."

— *author C JoyBell C*

We've all seen those images in the playground when two knobbly-kneed kids are being encouraged to fight, the crowd of eager onlookers clapping and shouting. Most people hate conflict or confrontation; they shy away from it. When I'm coaching, I often get asked how to manage conflict in a work situation. When I asked another coach the same question, she answered that with the right communication along the way, conflict will not occur. To some extent I agree. Sometimes you need to dig deep and resolve a situation and other times you just have to walk away.

The fact is we as people fear conflict, especially when it threatens upset to our lives and our tightly-controlled ecosystems. As an example, if your boss says to you without warning, "I'm going to change the reporting lines", meaning that in the future no one reports into you, what do you do?

I use the word "boss" for a reason because no natural leader would ever behave like this, but the world is filled with bosses and these situations happen. By boss I mean someone who has risen to a position of authority but has a fixed negative mindset, e.g. they constantly need to prove themselves, they get defensive, they always ignore critical feedback and are threatened by the success of others.

If you are a growth mindset person – someone who desires to learn and improve, is open to communication, embraces change, perseveres in the face of setbacks, learns from criticism, and finds lessons and inspiration in the success of others – you are going to struggle with this type of boss.

First Dig Deep

Tell them verbally and in writing how you feel and question whether you are really thriving in a fearful environment like this. As Maya Angelou said, "My mission in life is not merely to survive, but to thrive; and to do so with some passion, some compassion, some humor, and some style."

If this doesn't improve the situation, what can you do next? Complain to HR? Seek legal advice, and resign on the grounds of constructive dismissal? Or just walk away?

Walk Away

We fear conflict at work, it can paralyze us into a state of doing nothing. But doing nothing means that this time next year you will be in the same unfulfilling position as you are today. You have allowed the waves of life to wash over you and slam you onto the beach, unable to breathe. So, my advice would be to stop hanging on in there, waiting passively for things to change. Instead, pivot, turn and move towards something better.

The world of possibilities is waiting for you out there. Gather up all of your experience, your magic, plan for a new life and walk away. This time next year you will be in a totally different life, away from this toxic situation. This isn't losing, it is taking control of the things you can control. Believe me, you have won. Don't be that kid in the playground forced to stand and fight by the crowd even though it's not in your true nature or to your benefit.

Nothing is Ever Perfect (fear of presenting)

The first time I ever presented to a crowd of 1000 people was in big hall in Geneva when I was 28 years old. My creative director was poorly so he asked me to step in for him the day before the conference. I knew the presentation well, I'd helped write it – it was on *"Generous Brands"* and explored how businesses could be more generous, kind and helpful to customers.

The central idea of the talk was powerful and was already known to be a successful strategy for some of our clients, but it didn't always go down well with cash-strapped businesses struggling to be profitable. So, I was always quite nervous when my director presented it, let alone me.

"Oh," he said through his bad cold, "you will get marks out of 10 by the organisers, so do your best. I'm looking forward to hearing how you do!" He sniffed and hung up our call. I can honestly say my fear was overwhelming.

When Steve Jobs gave those epic talks, don't for one minute believe he had just walked out on stage. He practised relentlessly; he was legendary for his preparation. He would rehearse on stage for hours over many weeks prior to the launch of a major product. As a result, his presentations were delivered flawlessly. He knew every demo and font on each slide. By comparison, I had no time to prepare. Oh my, on that that flight to Geneva I can honestly say the FEAR was so enormous, at one point on the plane, yes, I'm ashamed to admit I hoped it would crash so I wouldn't have to give the speech. Wow! That's how bad the fear was!

I recorded the speech onto my phone and listened to it over and over in my earphones as I mouthed the words to myself. My fear kept telling me I didn't know the words, the projector wouldn't work, the images would be too small to see. As the plane dropped so did my stomach. The fear grew... 1000 people would hate me, the stage would be too high, the poor mark I would get from the organisers would ruin my career, I wouldn't be able to pay my rent, everything would be over, and I'd be doomed to years of unemployment and homelessness (my Fear Monster is a drama queen!).

After repeatedly mumbling the presentation like a mantra, I walked out onto the stage to face 1000 faces. Having a vivid imagination and remembering Steve Jobs saying "have fun", I Imagined the audience as kittens. Not just any kittens but cuddly ones with dopey eyes like *Puss in Boots*, played by Antonio Banderas, in the film *Shrek*.

I leant down to open my laptop, smiled to myself, and when I looked up there were a 1000 adorable kittens smiling back at me. They wanted me to do well, they had my back. I explained I'd stepped in for my boss and this was first big talk and they smiled even wider. I relaxed and recited the presentation word for word, without a hitch! What did I learn?

I learnt that when you are truly passionate about something, it ignites a sense of purpose and drive within you. This newly found enthusiasm helps to diminish feelings of fear or self-doubt, as your focus shifts from potential obstacles to the excitement of sharing something meaningful with others. Having a story to share can be powerful. Stories have the ability to captivate and inspire people, making the message more relatable and memorable. Keep nurturing your passion and sharing your voice – it's a remarkable way to create a positive impact on both yourself and those around you.

FEARLESS THINKING...

Be vulnerable. Tell your story.

Practice relentlessly.

Have fun! Let your imagination free.

Podcast recommendation: *How to Own the Room* by Viv Groskop

Jump In (fear of setting up a business)

I often get asked how I built two seven-figure businesses from start-up to sale (the first one I built with a friend, so I had help) . Only 2% of all female-led businesses achieve this level of annual revenue, so what made me part of that 2% success story? Did my journey start with FEAR? No! Was I fearful during the adventure? Well, at times…

For me, it started with love and passion for creativity. My curious creative itch, as I call it. When you love something, it doesn't feel like work, it feels like flying. Self-belief and self-love are difficult when a business rests on your shoulders but, as my non-exec mentor used to say, "A bit of fear makes you think a little bit harder, and that stops you falling over a proverbial cliff when things are going bad!"

At the beginning, I knew very little about setting up a business. Nor could I have imagined the fear, stress and strain that it would have on my mind, body and soul at points along the journey. At times, the business became a hungry animal and consumed most of my life and thinking. At other times it set me on fire with enthusiasm and made me feel fearless. Either way, the pace of growth was exponential. It made me feel real, alive, useful, curious, and at times scared to death at my lack of knowledge. When I once asked a top CEO how he got into that role, he said by experience. I asked how he got that experience, and he said by making mistakes. There it goes – we all do it! But if you don't try, isn't that worse than failing?

Diving in and setting up a business can create lots of fear. No PAYE monthly check, not always sure where the next pound will come from to feed the baby chicks, and hoping that you always provide excellent service for your clients so they keep coming back. Fearing less comes with practise, making mistakes, thinking fast on your feet and pivoting. Knowing that if you do your best then good things will happen. You do get paid, but it might be 50p or £500,000 and that's the "risk it for the biscuit" element, as my son would say. But I never feared change. Change kept me moving forward. I feared more standing still and not growing so in the end the one outweighed the other.

My people skills, finance skills, management, leadership, creative, PR and new business abilities took off when I set up the company. They were essential to its survival and anything that was essential I read about, digested, and actioned at a rapid pace. The hundreds of books I read helped me to grow quickly. There isn't a subject in the world that you can't research on the phone in your hand! I didn't stay stuck in old habits and "comfortable" places of no growth.

People say that I work too hard. I usually disagree. For me, it is all about how you define 'work' and what that work was. If it lights me up, helps me to learn and grow then it's not work, it's living life. Setting up businesses for me was living. Why? Well, for the most part it was enormous fun! Also, it taught me the fundamentals of this book.

FEARLESS THINKING...

Top business hacks to combat fear:

Hack 1: If you have an idea for a business write it down, anything in your head has no weight.

Book recommendation: *The Beermat Entrepreneur* by Chris West and Mike Southon, the first business book I ever read.

Hack 2: Read, read and read about any area you know nothing about until you become an expert. Or, ask an expert if you can't afford the time to become one yourself.

Tip: subscribe to *Blinkist* to understand books & podcasts in 15 minutes. Each blink gives you essential snippets of knowledge. If you love the blinks, buy the book. www.blinkist.com

Hack 3: You will never know if you don't try. I advise lots of people to make their new business idea into a side-hustle (Plan B) and carry on with their day job. When Plan B makes half as much as your current income, then jump to Plan B full-time. You will always make more money from profits than PAYE if you're driven by passion, not fear.

Hack 4: As Steven King says about writing novels, the same goes for setting up a business—it can be like driving down a foggy road with the headlights on, only seeing 1 metre ahead. Be ready, think quick, expect change, don't give in to fear and 'pivot, pivot, pivot' like Ross in *Friends*.

The Value of Time and Managing It (fear of time running out)

For a long-time, I pretended not to know that I only had one life to lead. When the awareness threatened to rise, I'd shove it back down. There was no point in admitting it as I couldn't change it. I was a mother, a business owner employing 68 people, a wife…I had responsibilities. I had amazing offices three minutes' walk from the River Thames and yet, in the six years I worked there, I'd never been down to the river and watched it flow. There was never enough time, or so it seemed.

When I first found out I had cancer, I went into work and told my staff. They were quiet, they didn't know what to say. They were scared for me and scared for themselves – this could mean change and people fear uncertainty. When I left the office unsure of what else to say, except to keep saying I was sorry for this, I walked down to the river on my own. The river was doing what it always did, it flowed. For hours I sat and watched it, wondering why I'd never been down there before. Its flow was hypnotic. Subconsciously I breathed in time with the splashes and slowly the panic I felt in my heart, the responsibility, the burden, the need to say sorry, all gradually subsided as I simply watched the water move.

I feel a little ashamed to say that as I sat there wondering what chemotherapy would be like, I was looking desperately for some kind of silver lining and finding none. I knew I had to reduce my hours at work to make time for treatment. I satisfied myself with the commitment to managing my time better. I would no longer go round and round on the carousel but choose how to spend my time more carefully. At least it felt good to have some sort of positive outlook moving forward. Yes, I was super fearful, but the fear of death had been my wake up call. Today, my life/work balance is more important than ever.

As a society we have never been more teched up, more connected and yet more lonely and burned out. To survive we need to become more aware, more intuitive, and self-examining. We need to harness our natural gifts and be less reliant on the machine. We've all seen the stats of our daily phone usage and shuddered.

Ask yourself, that 4- 5 hours spent each day texting, chatting, emailing – is it worth it? Businesspeople talk about the "opportunity cost" of doing things. What else could you do with this time that would be more profitable?

Where have your dreams gone, have they been pushed aside, was there no time for them? We've all tried to justify that use of screen time to ourselves e.g., Kindle reading, work emails, texting and organising our social diaries. But we cannot deceive ourselves. Do we need to set ourselves a limit?

Our minds might need to keep busy, busy, busy but our bodies need to rest. So, think about what you do with your time now, dig deep and find the answers. If you worry about what you do with your time, then start to measure it and plan it.

FEARLESS THINKING...

What do you do with your time?

Keep a diary of your time usage per week and see where it goes.

e.g., how many hours do you spend on your phone, at work, with the kids, socialising etc.

Could you use your time more wisely?

Could you plan your time better and in a more balanced way?

Choose the Right Path

Everyone is so busy these days. They sometimes lose the ability to stop, think and weigh up the right way ahead. They are content to follow , not considering whether that path leads them to a place they want to go.

Once we start along a path, we feel compelled to continue. We resist the urge to turn back and retrace our steps. As if turning back means we made bad decisions and we can't admit it.

No amount of job security is worth suffering being lead down a path that has killed off your dreams. You only have one life so don't waste time chasing a dead end. If you feel anxiety, depression, anger, blame, grief, or resentment, watch your step – you could be on the wrong path! The right choice will make you stronger.

Pushchair Panic (fear of being a bad mom)

"If you want to change the world, first change yourself, then tell others how you did it. Never demand that people change. Inspire them to change using your own change as an example instead."

— Dan Pearce, Single Dad Laughing

I woke up in a panic – I was late. I raced around, got my three-year-old son ready, dropped him off at the nursery, walked on to the tube station, travelled 12 stations standing up, walked a few blocks, up three floors in an elevator and into work. Only then did I realise that I was still pushing my son's buggy! I hadn't dropped it off at the push chair shed at his nursery. What was the first thing I did – laugh, blush, cry, swear? No, I felt panic...because for a moment I expected my boy to be still sitting there in the buggy.

Love can often be ultimately realised in its truest, purest form when you see your first child. After the incredible surge and outpouring of love, I was instantly filled with fear that I would not be able to protect my son. This tiny baby, with his thick black hair snuggled in a blanket. His blue eyes, just visible through tiny slits in his eyelids, were like a carefully cut decorations on a fine pastry or cake. His tiny mouth was perfectly formed to make gentle cooing sounds that called out to my heart and captivated my mind, pulling me in. Everyone is different, but as soon as I saw his face that first time, my mind started down the guilt path.

Leaving my little boy with someone else while I went to work was one of the hardest things I have had to do. I felt guilty returning to work when he was 11-months old, guilt at leaving him with my mom at times when I needed a break, guilt at putting him to bed 15 minutes early because I was exhausted, and this guilt never stopped. Three years later, I still had difficulty letting go of his pushchair!

My response to the guilt when I was in my 30s was to work harder and harder to contribute more and more, to counterbalance the guilt until I wore myself thin. I went into machine-mode and disconnected from my inner nature. My sons are now 12 and 17 and neither has any recollection or notion of the thousands of nursery drop offs, the tears I cried at the door, the sprint from the station or the many times I felt that I was a rubbish mom. They remember me for being there for them when they needed me, cuddling them when they wanted a squeeze, helping them with their homework, standing at the back row of the school play, which I'd just managed to arrive in time for. The guilt I placed on myself didn't help me at all – it was a gradual erosion of my inner harmony that I'd allowed to set in that served no purpose to anyone, including myself.

The Spare Body (fear of ageing)

I wished for a while that I could open the wardrobe and pass the baton to a pristine other version of myself. One with no scars, no double mastectomy, no fat, no wrinkles, no saggy areas, no bumps or pimples. Just perfect. I've read many self-help books and tried many diets to keep living longer. Vegan diets, raw green juices, intermittent fasting, Atkins, Palm Beach, paleo, low protein, high protein, only grilled protein and boiled rice, no red meat, no carbs or alcohol, no sugar, no additives, no GMO, no pesticides, free-range, no dairy, no stress, no way baby. These days I get most inspiration from two of my favourite books on the subject.

The first is *The Blue Zone*: Lessons for living Longer From the People Who've lived the Longest, by Dan Buettner. It explores the regions around the world where people tend to live much longer than the global average. In these regions, or Blue Zones, people commonly reach ages of 100 or more and have lower incidence of chronic diseases like heart disease, diabetes, and certain cancers. The book delves into the lifestyles, diets, social structure, and cultural factors that contribute to the remarkable longevity and wellbeing of the people in these areas. Key factors and lessons highlighted in the book include: eating a plant-based diet, regular low-intensity physical activities, building strong social bonds and community involvement, strategies for stress reduction, having a clear sense of purpose, strong family relationships and an active lifestyle walking and gardening. Everything is holistic and interconnected.

The second book is about the lifestyle concept of *Ikigai: The Japanese Secret to a Long and Happy Life* by Hector Garcia and Francesc Miralles. *Ikigai* means "a reason to live' or a reason to jump out of bed in the morning. It's the place where your needs, desires, ambitions, and satisfaction meet – a place of balance and a secret recipe for a long and happy life. Key concepts and takeaways from the book include: aligning your passions with your purpose to lead a fulfilling life, being present and mindful, living a balanced lifestyle (integrated work, leisure, social interactions and self-care), maintaining a healthy diet and physical activity, cultivating strong meaningful relationships and continuously growing and learning.

Trust me, these books, they do massively help. But the fact is we will grow older, and nobody has found a reliable way around that yet. Your face and skin will wrinkle, your body will weaken, but your soul will always be beautiful. Is that enough or is the fear of aging so strong that we absolutely, definitely, must need to nip, tuck, Botox, fill in, suck out, lift, contour, enlarge or reduce? Look, it's everyone's prerogative to decide what to do with their body, my only advice is to consider the side effects.

A nutritionist friend put the premature birth of my baby and then the cancer down to overworking. She joked that I needed two bodies to maintain the pace I had set myself in life. Then, more seriously, she chided me – surely two warnings are enough? A spare body in the wardrobe suddenly seemed like an enviable thing to have. But I realised that my body is my history. Every scar, line, and wrinkle marks a chapter in my life. Now I smile in the mirror because I survived everything that has been thrown at me. I smile because when I was knocked down, I always got back up.

FEARLESS THINKING…

Take a pause and focus on yourself:

What can you thank your body for doing for you this week?

Try to feel grateful for your good health or, if you are unwell, for the things that your body does do well.

Money, Money, Money (fear of financial ruin)

"Money, money, money. Must be funny. In the rich man's world. Money, money, money. Always sunny. In the rich man's world."

—ABBA song lyrics, written by Benny Andersson and Björn Ulvaeus

I get it, it's a massive fear. It's one of the biggest for people that I coach. Most people hide their head in the sand like an ostrich and don't face financial difficulties at all.

Take the first step and read *The Richest Man in Babylon* by George Clason. It's a classic from 1926 but is still in print today because of its timeless wisdom. It dispenses financial advice through a collection of parables set 4000 years ago in ancient Babylon. At that time, Babylon was the wealthiest city on the planet, with terraced gardens so beautiful they were one of the Seven Wonders of the Ancient World.

Honestly, the advice is still so relevant and valuable today, I have achieved financial security and prepared for a comfortable future by following those parables!

A summary of his book in three sentences is:

1. Save at least 10% of everything you earn and do not confuse your necessary expenses with your desires (needs vs wants).

2. Work hard to improve your skills and keep them up to date because wealth is the result of a reliable income stream.

3. You cannot arrive at the fullest measure of success until you crush the spirit of procrastination within you (don't put important work off, do it today).

This is sound advice, as I found out to my benefit. When my son was born, I started putting some money aside for his education fund every month. Now he is 17 there is enough money to send him to university. Back then, I remember being a bit cynical, but here I am today thanking *the Richest Man in Babylon*. The cover price of the book was modest, but the value of its contents is beyond measure.

What each person calls their "necessary expenses" will always grow to match their income unless that urge to splurge is resisted. Do not confuse your necessary expenses with your desires. I make sure my monthly commitments and savings are covered before deciding how much of my pay cheque is for spending. If my income increases, so do my savings!

Earlier I talked about learning and growing. If you want to increase your ability to earn, then first improve your skills. As you perfect your craft, your ability to earn more increases. The more we know, the more we may earn.

Do not live beyond your means. If you are in debt and are able to, live on 70% of what you make. Save 10% for yourself. Use the remaining 20% to repay your debts. Stick with the plan. Money accrues surprisingly quickly, and debts reduce with discipline and consistency. Making regular payments and avoiding defaults will improve your credit score too.

FEARLESS THINKING…

Make a note of all your monthly expenses and monthly income.

Review and calculate all your debts.

Add the monthly debt re-payments to the monthly expenses.

See what the difference is between your total expenses and income.

If your expenses outweigh your income, then you need to spend less or find ways to increase your income. This is where it helps that you have a note of all your monthly expenses. Choose which things you can do without next month.

You might benefit from a financial review with a qualified professional. Seek advice from the bank or a legally approved financial advisor. Don't put your head in the sand, get help today.

The Diamond in the Coal (from the bad thing we fear, some good can spring)

It can be so difficult at times to see the light in a dark situation, but I promise it's there. "Find the diamond in the coal," I was told by a counsellor. "I know your situation is difficult, but good things will come out of this, like finding a diamond in a coal." But it wasn't easy.

In the space of six months everything had changed. I was told I had a 75% chance of dying within the next five years, my best friend and business partner ended our business and inadvertantly our life long-friendship, I was struggling with my 15-month-old son, I'd been through six gruelling chemo sessions, lost my hair and been pushed into an early menopause.

My panic attacks were so bad I was struggling to breathe and sleep at night. My life was out of control. Every part of it had changed overnight. My health, my business, my mindset, my best friendship, my family life. It felt my whole inner and outer world was in one big meltdown.

One night, I lay on the bathroom floor and cried out for help.

I realised the hard truth that I was going to die one day – maybe not in my 30s but my odds were not looking good. In my race through life, there had been no plan. I'd been falling and grasping at whatever came my way. My creativity and my true nature had been hidden. The thought of me dying when I had not really lived was overwhelming, and desperately sad. I couldn't hide my fear, I was scared to death. I had a 15-month-old baby and a husband to love, friends to make memories with and a life-long dream of being an author to realise. This wasn't my time. But an important fact of life was suddenly crystal clear. One day we all die...

With this new inner sense of my mortality, how could I go back to my old life? I felt that I'd learnt and accepted life's biggest lesson. I felt a rising need to share my understanding – but was it something others would want to know?

I went in search of answers and reached deep into my soul, body, and mind to find my true nature, *"the diamond in the coal".* All those dreams that I'd tucked away for my retirement that now might not happen. They needed to be written down, given meaning and purpose and acted upon. I needed to change. I needed to take control of my mindset, my health, my income, friendships, dreams, to trust my instincts and to stop living in fear of what might never happen.

So, I looked closely at my inner mind/landscape, my thoughts, words, beliefs and ultimately my destiny, like I'm asking you to do now. I decided to STOP, to learn, to grow, to embrace and change. To choose my nights out and my friends more wisely, to bring my dreams to life and live in a wilder, more instinctive way.

If you work hard enough on your inner self, spend time to understand yourself, your energy, your moods, your triggers, and your joys, you will always be able to understand and learn more about your own pain and how to handle it. You will move forward. My diamond in the coal is that I could have woken up at 90 not having lived this life fully. I could have worked a million hours and never stopped to breathe or admire the rising and setting sun. Being forced to stop, weigh things up and understand the value of life helped me to realise that every minute is a blessing. I'd found my diamond in the coal and for that I am truly grateful. That's why I'm writing this book – I want you to find yours too.

Stop Numbing the Fear

What is numbing? It's turning attention away, tuning out, switching off. It's when you can't or won't sit in your own skin and accept your reality.

Common ways to numb pain and hide it from your conscious awareness:

Drugs (pretending)

Alcohol (forgetting)

Sugar (masking)

Hard core exercise

Social Media

Shopping

Sex

Self-harm

Food (over-eating vs starvation)

Anger (a stronger emotion)

Depression (numbing all emotion)

Why do we numb our fear? Because it's way too painful. You don't want to think about painful things, so you numb them out. In times of deep despair, the first thing I must do is stop drinking alcohol. Drinking is forgetting – drowning my sorrow, my thoughts, my brain, and my mind. Swimming in mud. The wine is only followed by a morning of despair, depression, and anxiety. As painful as it is, I must sit with myself in a sober state and meditate. Numbing your fear just kicks the can down the road.

Pushing through fear into a fear-less life means NOT numbing. And note I say "fear-less" not "fearless"; there is a big distinction. We all need a little bit of fear for survival. Fear makes us pivot, alert, conscious, on guard but TOO much fear and we become paralysed, unable to move, change, compute or adapt. We stick to predictability, like a person holding on for life to a cliff edge.

Change is inevitable, but it can be painful. Pain creates change. The process of profound change is akin to a caterpillar transforming into a butterfly. The process might seem daunting as the caterpillar enters a cocoon and undergoes a radical shift, but through this struggle, it emerges as a beautiful butterfly, prepared to explore new horizons. This experience generates a profound awareness that can be startling. When you emerge on the other side of challenging change, you reassemble and become whole once more. You exist in a different form and context, with largely the same ingredients – just seasoned with a little more wisdom.

Numb yourself at your peril. A very close friend escaped to Canada one year after a break-up; it was her way to escape the pain. I remember her father fetching an old suitcase from their attic and the sounds of my friend and her mom crying. Her parents didn't drink alcohol, so her constant hangovers and drunken behaviour wasn't going down that well. Naively I asked her on a phone call a few weeks later if she was happy, but she laughed nervously and said, "That blue suitcase not only brought all my clothes but all my problems and traumas too. I didn't leave them at home; they came with me. There is no escaping or numbing them but I've stopped drinking and that makes me feel a whole heap better."

Life Hacks to Stop the Numbing

Life Hack 1: One drink is too many but a thousand not enough

I stopped drinking alcohol entirely for one year because I was not drinking for pleasure but as a prop for life. It had to stop. It was easy to drown in alcohol and drink away my pain, but it stopped me being creative, really living, awake, thinking, and helping myself. It filled my body and mind with poison that was the opposite of helping me.

Website recommendation: https://soberandsocial.com

Life Hack 2: Food is fuel

I look at what I'm eating and ask, "Is this fuelling me, is it giving my billion cells something good?" I keep a diary of what I'm eating and write in red all the food that is not fuelling my body e.g., the chocolate, the cream cakes, the egg custards. Then I write down in green all the bits that are fuelling me e.g., the vegetables, the fruits, the nuts, all the foods that are closer to nature and make my body more alkaline.

Book recommendations:

Anticancer: A new way of life, by David Servan-Schreiber. Yes, it says cancer but don't be put off – I wish I'd read this book in my 20s way before my diagnosis.

How not to die: Discover the foods scientifically proven to prevent and reverse disease, by Michael Greger MD.

Life Hack 3: Juicing makes a massive difference to your mind

I juice and fast for a few days each month to let my body detox and relax (60% of all our energy goes on digesting food) and eat only between 10am-7pm to give myself 16 hours a night of fasting. With it comes a clarity of thought that is so powerful. Out of the mental clarity arise new possibilities that bring me out of the fear zone into a calm space of self-belief and love for myself.

Book recommendation:

Juice Master Keeping It Simple: Over 100 Delicious Juices and Smoothies, by Jason Vale.

The 5:2 Cookbook: 100 Recipes for Fasting, by Angela Dowden.

Life Hack 4: Run wild

I walk in the park with nature and get back to my roots, touch the trees, walk bare foot in the grass and ground myself. Earthing or grounding means connecting with the energy of the planet beneath your feet and being fully present to experience the solidity of the here and now. This natural energy of the earth fills your mind, heart and soul and connects you with the universal power of nature.

Book recommendation: *Earthing: The Most Important Health Discovery Ever,* by Clinton Ober, Martin Zucker and Stephen Sinatra.

Life Hack 5: Calmness that comes from meditation

"If we transform our mind, everything we experience is transformed."

— *Yongey Mingyur Rinpoche*

Yongey Mingyur is a Tibetan meditation master who overcame chronic anxiety and panic attacks to transform his own life. He says that meditation brings with it an awareness of your mind, body, and soul, a connection with today and the now – and with that comes hope. If you live in the day you live in hope. If you are thinking and worrying about tomorrow that can bring with it a thousand fears of things that are possible but might never happen.

It seems so simple but, in a day of meditation, I feel more in control. In a few days my skin looks brighter, and my mind is more positive. Within 10 days I feel resilient, and my inner soul is searching for more.

Book recommendation:

The Joy of Living: Unlocking the Secret and Science of Happiness, by Mingyur Rinpoche.

Online meditation classes: The Joy of Living: https://joy.tergar.org

Fearless Thinking…

Take a pause and focus on yourself and write yourself a lifestyle diary…

LIFESTYLE DIARY:

Alcohol units per day, per week, per month:

Books read per day, per week, per month:

Exercise per day, per week, per month:

Moving From Fear (put on your big girl's pants and change the channel)

"First comes courage, then confidence, then success."

— *Jacqueline Gold, CBE, Gold Group International, Ann Summers and Knickerbox*

Jacqueline Gold was a dear friend, mentor, and a prime example of how a woman can rise from adversity to create an industry-defining, global chain of businesses. She taught me so much. Together we often discussed the importance of developing a positive attitude and believing in the power of change. Jacqueline didn't procrastinate; she actioned change. She used change to look for the potential and the possibilities to fuel a brighter future.

We all understand the desperate need to create change some days for ourselves. We want and crave the change but can't. But let me tell you a secret. You are in charge – you are holding the remote control in your hand. Don't let fear take a hold. There are many situations that we can't change through no fault of our own, so let them go! Stop trying to control the uncontrollable.

I cannot control the death of a loved one, when someone at work leaves, or when the world is in the middle of a pandemic. But there are lots of things I can control: who I work for, what I read, who I'm friends with, how I handle myself at work. They are all within my power to change. (I have created an exercise to help you with this later).

During some of the days when my illness had me feeling like I was falling apart, I'd find solace in simple tasks. Looking out of the window, meticulously making my bed with crisp, white sheets, folding dish towels, even sorting the big forks from the little ones – these acts of cleaning and tidying helped restore a semblance of order in my life. Amid a whirlwind of worries, my mind would spiral in tiny circles. Fear seemed intertwined with death, death seemed intertwined with fear. It was fine not to know how to proceed; self-forgiveness was key. At that point, I hadn't delved into the inner work that my life demanded. I used to believe that change revolved around external aspects – wealth, material possessions. However, I came to realise that true change originates from within. It's the inner realm that harbours the potential for transformation and the energy needed for change.

Now when I feel overwhelmed, I start with something simple, like saying to myself, *"I have the controller in my hand. I have control over so many things."*

Or, as Jacqueline Gold would say, *"Put on your big girl's pants and look for the amazing possibilities that could come through change."*

FEARLESS THINKING…

Move from a place of fear into fearing-less.

Now, as scary as it is, allow yourself to imagine a new world with you in it. Imagine in a year's time where you would like to be.

What are the three things you'd like to change that are in your control to change?

1.

2.

3.

The Antidote to FEAR (don't give in to despair, turn to self-love)

"I tell you, hopeless grief is passionless;
That only men incredulous of despair,
Half-taught in anguish, through the midnight air,
Beat upwards to God's throne in loud access
Of shrieking and reproach. Full desertness
In souls, as countries, lieth silent—bare
Under the blanching, vertical eye-glare
Of the absolute heavens."

— *Elizabeth Barrett Browning*

How do you know you are in despair? For me it is when I feel very little connection with anything. No rage or pain. In despair I feel like I am trapped behind a window just looking on as everyone gets on with their lives. And that makes me feel hopeless.

With cancer at times comes deep despair and hopelessness, a feeling that nothing that you do can make a difference. Like a waking nightmare, as terrible things are happening, your usual self-will and determination cannot aid you, any hope resides in other people helping you (your doctors). There is no guarantee of recovery, but people expect you to keep your energy and be upbeat about the situation.

As the philosopher Nietzsche said, "Some situations are so bad that to remain sane is insane." But, as with cancer and many major illnesses, you might look okay from the outside, so people forget.

To combat the feelings of despair, isolation, and hopelessness, you must learn that self-love is essential – the deep emotional, psychological, and spiritual growth type of self-love. I didn't put mine off until I had some peace, I doubled down and worked hard on my growth. I really focused on my aims, what I wanted from my life, where I was headed. I searched deeply, looked into my soul and asked myself, "What do I want out of my life, how can I turn my problem into possibilities for growth?"

Survival wasn't my plan – growth was. I wanted to be far better than before my illness, so I asked, "What does my mini universe look like to guide my growth? What goal or reason is there to believe that my life moving forward will be better?"

What did "better" mean? Different, more unique, more reflective of my true self so that I can make my 30 trillion cells smile and my immune system stronger? This is the key, and every day I ask myself those same questions to keep focused.

If you reflect and use this book as a tool to work towards a meaningful life goal, it will change how you fundamentally feel. Thinking fear-less will feel wealthier and healthier, you will feel less helpless, less like you are always reacting to life's challenges and that you can make those challenges into opportunities for growth. You are actively fighting to sing your song, to have your voice heard, and since this helps you physically, you will start to break out of your nightmare of despair, and you will find your power. If you have a goal, then you have a purpose. As Nietzsche wrote, "He who has a why to live for can bear almost any how."

NOW TAKE ACTION!

Keep these truths close to your heart

1/ Awareness of your fears is to acknowledge them and deal with them.
2/ With action you can navigate fear, otherwise it will cause paralysis.
3/ Don't let fear be the driver. Be aware of it and make it the passenger.
4/ Fear of the future is seven times worse than the reality when you get there. Thought is a powerful thing so keep your mind in the here and now but with one eye on your plan.
5/ You can't change things beyond your control so focus on the changes you do have power over.
6/ Fear leads to anxiety, a weakened immune system, and potential illness
7/ Turn all frustration into fascination; it helps shift your perspective on life.
8/ Seek assistance from others. Surround yourself with individuals you share profound connections with.
9/ Learn when to delve into challenges and when to step away from toxic situations.
10/ Craft a plan to anchor something substantial in your mind (your guiding North Star, as I elaborate on later)
11/ If you worry about what you do with your time, measure it and plan it.

12/ Work out what traps you in life and don't let yourself be put in a cage.
13/ Guilt-ridden mothers serve no purpose to anyone.
14/ Every scar, line, or wrinkle marks a chapter in your life.
15/ Read *The Richest Man in Babylon* for tried and trusted money advice.
16/ Find your diamond in the coal in a fearful situation and move forward.
17/ Numbing your fear just kicks the can down the road. Face it!
18/ You have the controller to your life in your hand so if you don't like what's happening change the channel!
19/ We are "a long time dead", as my twelve-year-old once said, so act today!
20/ Self-love is a healing force. Embrace a growth mindset.

FEARLESS WOMEN Jacqueline Gold CBE

"It doesn't matter how old you are, how successful you are, or how privileged you are; it doesn't change the fact that you experience challenges along the way. For me, I never wanted to feel like a victim. I always wanted to gain something from a negative experience. I always look for the positive that comes out of any challenging, fearful situation."

— Jacqueline Gold CBE

In February 2023, mere weeks before her unexpected passing, I had the privilege of spending time with Jacqueline, engaging in discussions about this book and conducting an interview with her. She wholeheartedly supported the project and possessed a profound understanding of the significance of authentic wealth and health.

Jacqueline was a highly accomplished businesswoman and the executive chair of Gold Group International. In 2016 she was awarded a CBE for her services to entrepreneurship, women in business and social enterprises and she rightly earned the nickname Warrior Woman, for her ability to navigate challenging circumstances, including a breast cancer diagnosis. She also suffered the devastating loss of her baby son when he was eight months old.

Despite the hardships, Jacqueline, her family (including her father David and sister Vanessa), and her team built a nine-figure business. Balancing this responsibility with raising her surviving twin daughter, she remained an optimistic leader and consistently discovered silver linings and lessons within adversity.

As she rose to the position of Chairwomen, Jacqueline had to overcome gender prejudices, discrimination, sexism, harassment, and even threats (she once received a bullet in the post). She championed female and sexual empowerment, helping many women become financially independent. She established WOW Women, a support network for women in business, which grew to include thousands of members, from small start-ups to multimillion-pound businesses.

Jacqueline firmly believed in continuous learning and growth, staying curious, and seeking inspiration from people and life experiences. Despite appearing shy on the surface, she possessed unwavering confidence, ambition, and a burning passion to empower others. She always emphasised that passion and courage came first, leading to confidence and amazing accomplishments when individuals step outside their comfort zone.

Despite facing skepticism from a male-dominated board in the early days regarding women's interest in sex, she consistently heeded her customers' voices and fearlessly expanded her business, resulting in substantial growth. Amid the challenges of the Covid pandemic, her business encountered significant hurdles. Nevertheless, her team exceeded expectations, achieving remarkable outcomes. The Ann Summers party sales ambassadors experienced exponential growth within a matter of months, providing much-needed financial support to women. This success can be attributed to a creative and empowering business model.

Jacqueline's health journey was not without its difficulties. It brought her face-to-face with her emotional vulnerability and the need for emotional support. Despite being perceived as strong and resilient, she bravely opened to close friends and confided in them about her struggles. This willingness to be vulnerable allowed her to forge deeper connections with others and nurtured an environment of understanding and empathy.

Through this journey, Jacqueline nurtured a fresh curiosity and a profound longing to meditate, embrace daily gratitude, and foster personal growth, gaining a genuine appreciation for health. This internal exploration unveiled a heightened wisdom and an intensified appreciation for the profound depth of friendship and love with those dearest to her. She often expressed that her ultimate happiness in life originated from the deep connections she shared with her family and friends. She firmly believed in the importance of discovering one's tribe (comprising friends, family, and networking community), nurturing profound love, and cherishing the individuals who hold utmost significance.

Her legacy was truly profound, and she will forever be associated with female empowerment. Her dedication to supporting women's financial independence left a lasting impact on the lives of countless individuals. Her inspiring journey, coupled with her fearless approach to business and life, serves as a beacon for women aspiring to succeed in male-dominated industries.

"Have courage, but you can never have enough of it, so be daring! Be engaging, be confident, and don't follow the norm. Make sure you build your network in business, make it a natural part of your life. Every time you walk into a room full of strangers, there could be an opportunity there that could change your life!"

— Jacqueline Gold CBE

Jacqueline's three tips for managing fear

Shared with me during our discussions for this book, these tips reflect Jacqueline's fearless and empowering approach to life and business, inspiring others to overcome challenges and achieve their goals.

1. "**Create a plan**": Jacqueline believed in the power of setting clear goals and creating plans to achieve them. Each year, she would establish specific objectives aligned with her passions, such as empowering women in the bedroom, supporting women in business, and in her later years promoting integrative and complementary medicine without barriers to aid health journeys. She emphasised the importance of starting with small ideas that can grow big, always pushing boundaries, and being open to new possibilities. "But all businesses have to be commercial for them to get attention, through advertising, a strong platform, or a podcast," she told me. "Or people don't take it seriously."
2. "**Put on your big girl's pants,**" she would tell me a few times when I struggled with a situation; I loved this advice. She often said that confronting challenges was occasionally necessary for personal and professional growth. Jacqueline encouraged individuals not to shy away from difficult conversations that can help move them forward. She believed in embracing one's power and realising that they are stronger than they may realise.
3. **"Look for the positive in challenging situations"** Jacqueline's ability to find positives in any difficult or fearful circumstance was central to her resilience and success. She understood that focusing on ambition,

staying curious, and embracing new opportunities for growth was vital for personal development. She was a crusader for positivity and believed in empowering women to be their best selves and work towards positive cultural changes.

STEP 2: Moving from Fear to Love

The power of love. Love expands. Love heals and creates new possibilities. Love is infinite and operates on a higher frequency of universal hope and energy. The feeling of love lifts and lights you up and makes you feel that anything is possible.

Fear makes our perspective small; it inhibits wisdom, guidance and direction. It limits your life and confuses your mind. When we doubt, we lose hope and faith in ourselves. Fear is how we lose our mind and our inner peace. It fights the problem but isn't the solution. We need to move beyond this and find love for ourselves.

When we become aware of our actions and intentions we can start walking towards self-love. Moving from fear to self-love helps you to find a real solution, to change your vibration and place yourself outside of the problem and expands your awareness into a world of possibilities.

It is important to really take a good look at what self-love means. We are taught that vanity and arrogance are bad qualities. Self-love doesn't mean vanity nor arrogance. It means being honest and realistic about our strengths (not just our weaknesses), being compassionate to ourselves, learning from our mistakes and allowing ourselves to dream of better things, because that is how we learn and grow. Love operates at a high and powerful frequency that helps us to flow, grow and learn. Look inwards and find your inner voice, let your heart guide you and connect you to yourself and your own personal growth journey. Love is the power that will pull you into the future without fear.

Step 2 focuses on the inner you. Understanding you is a fundamental thing that can help you better navigate the world and to make good use of the people and resources you find there. If you tap into the natural energy of you, self-love will flow. Learning to love yourself no matter what isn't easy. Taking the time to pay attention to your inner knowing – instincts, hunches, and innate knowledge of which you can't quite trace the root. Your intuition sends you messages or compels you to do certain things, like take a different route home or call up an old friend you haven't seen in a while. It can quietly tell you if somebody you've just met is good or bad news. Power can be found in the sense of self-love, knowledge, autonomy, and alignment that comes from trusting your intuition. It comes from knowing that you are connecting with and being spiritually guided by the trustworthy voice of your higher self – your own self-love. Having a stronger intuition can enable you to feel more empowered and assured in making personal, emotional decisions and simply navigating everyday life. Why waste energy fretting? Dare to love, to dream, focus on what you are doing today to bring about a positive change tomorrow!

A Head full of Bees (be aware of your worries and capture them)

"Confusion is the beginning of understanding, the first stage of letting go of the neuronal gossip, that used to keep you chained to very specific ideas about who you are and what you are capable of, confusion in other words is the first step on the path to real well being."

– Yongey Mingyur Rinpoche

Like you, I have millions of thoughts per day. Each thought is a bee buzzing busily in my brain, wanting to be heard. If I'm not careful, I allow the thoughts to run wild in my mind till my head feels like it's full of bees! These are the days when I struggle to be logical, the days when I allow each bad thought to fly through my mind, uncontrolled. Each bee a single negative voice, buzzing loudly and relentlessly. "I'm overwhelmed. I'm trapped. I'm afraid!"

When the bees have full control, I'm helpless. Fear feels like death approaching, but I'm not ready to die, so I panic. The panic rises and becomes a stone in my chest, stopping my breath. The bees are smothering me with negativity.

The bees (my inner fearful thoughts) say, "You are not good enough! You will fail, your work will run out and you won't have any money. Then you will lose your home. What will happen to your family without a house? Your children are gaming too much and haven't done their homework. Your husband hasn't looked at you with loving eyes for ages, is he going to leave? Your friend hasn't called – is she upset with you? Is your cancer back? The client at work looks sad today—maybe you have disappointed her? You're too fat, too wrinkled, your face is sagging in old age, you're going to be poor, your house needs a clean, buzz, buzz, buzz!"

I've learned that when I resolutely confront the fear or problem, I can take away its power. I turn my worry bees (my inner fearful thoughts) into a list that I can see and reflect on. Instead of seeing these as my worst fears, I look to see if I can turn them into opportunities for growth. Awareness brings about a new beginning.

Fearless thinking...

Exercise 1: Imagine all your fears as buzzing bees and randomly write your top fears in the body of the bees. Become aware of them, name them.
When you look at the bees you will see that there are many worries, under many areas of your life and with varying degrees of urgency.

Exercise 2: Capture your bees.

"A man is but a product of his thoughts. What he thinks he becomes."

—Gandhi

Take a blank piece of paper. Take all the words you put in the bees and group them into the five key areas:

1/ **Financial**: money issues

2/ **Mental**: mental health + spirituality

3/ **Physical**: my health/well-being

4/ **Social**: my tribe/relationships with family and friends.

5/ **Time**: what do I do with my time?

Start thinking about these five areas one at a time first, rather than feeling overwhelmed.

Then look at this list of big fears and see if you can turn any of them into challenges or opportunities for growth. Ask yourself, how will things look in five years' time? These issues are some great opportunities for growth, so, where am I going in life? Where do I want to be? What do I want to achieve?

We Are Remarkable (and don't forget it!)

Often there is so much pain in our own hearts that we defeat ourselves with doubt, judgment, and self-loathing. Going through this pain and surviving will enrich your inner life. It is difficult when you are down and must build yourself back up again, but you get to experience the whole universe of emotions and that brings wisdom and resilience. As J.K Rowling famously said, "Rock bottom became the solid foundation on which I rebuilt my life."

Remember, as human beings we are remarkable and we can achieve extraordinary things. Human beings can turn weeds into gardens, imagination into landscapes, ideas into businesses. Reach down inside yourself and become remarkable. Start today to change tomorrow. Reconnect with your own natural energy; be more instinctive and achieve remarkable things.

Living in less fear creates a space in your mind to explore where you can "full fill" your true potential. Make it your quest to find your inner self and your own uniqueness, develop your purpose and find your tribe of people who will help you to materialise your dream.

The Idiot (delete the bad inner talk)

"I am a stupid idiot!" my husband said out loud one day when he was on a coaching course. Everyone on the class looked up, startled. He told me later that it had just popped out of his mouth, voicing one of his inner voices (or bees) that he usually kept to himself. Low in energy and mood, he had let it slip out and so he apologised to the group for his embarrassing outburst.

Half an hour later and much to the surprise of the room, the tutor suddenly shouted at him, "You're really stupid, aren't you? Ha, what a stupid idiot you are!"

"I bristled," he said. "How dare she speak to me like that – but I was so shocked that I just sat in silence with my mouth open, while the rest of the group looked on in amazement."

"Well isn't that just what you called yourself?" said the tutor. "Isn't that how you described yourself earlier in front of everyone here? I wonder, why would you ever say that to yourself about yourself?" Then she looked him in the eye, "You know, you should choose your words and thoughts more carefully, in case you start to believe them."

I felt a sharp sadness and compassion for him as he told me this story because I knew he had been through such a tough time recently (leaving his own business and looking for a new career, while I was battling cancer and we had two young children). He was upset with himself for needing to make a career move at a difficult time and he was doubting what he had to offer to the world. From my perspective, what he gave to me was immeasurable. He had been my rock and support when I was critically ill, the one who held my hand in the middle of the night when I had nightmares and panic attacks, the person who never looked at me with anything other than love, hope and determination. Without him there were times I'd have drowned in sadness and never started the journey towards a new life, yet he was filled with self-loathing!

Negative self-talk is something we all engage in. But doing it makes you feel more helpless and less motivated. If only we could see ourselves the way others see us.

I Love Myself (make all your words of hope and love, not fear)

I travelled to Northern India to spend 10 days meditating at the Palpung Sherabling monastery. It has 250 monks' quarters that accommodate over 500 monks, three shrine halls, six shrine rooms, and all of the traditional and modern monastic features. Palpung Sherabling also has retreat houses for visitors from around the world, as well as individual cabins for lay practitioners. The 12th Kenting Tai Situpa, the Buddhist leader who founded the monastery and its university, was running the meditation sessions that I attended over the 10 days. He spent his day educating masters and practitioners of the next generation. I was lucky to be invited to stay.

During one of his numerous talks, Tai Situpa shared his surprise upon traveling to the West and discovering that many people there didn't hold a strong self-appreciation. He conveyed with pride, "I love myself," repeating it multiple times to ensure its profound impact on us. He was shocked that so many people took antidepressants and needed therapy, had eating disorders, drank to excess or took drugs. He could not understand why people would need or want to numb their minds, bodies and emotions in ways that are harmful to their health. He was amazed that so many people were unhappy with their lives. He never thought that people would choose jobs that made them so stressed and unwell that they would require medical treatment or even hospitalisation. He believed that if a person truly loved themself, they would not choose actions or lifestyles that harmed their body or mind.

In the West, the concept of loving ourselves often becomes associated with appearance or arrogance. Consequently, substantial sums are spent on cosmetic surgery, beauty products, fashion, and the latest gadgets or cars. We work until we drop just to accumulate expensive possessions, only to throw them out when something shinier catches our eye. We might love the illusion we project, the face we wear, but we don't know or cherish or love our true inner selves.

Tai Situpa explained that he has compassion, love, and only kindness for himself, so he chooses to live in a way that brings him inner peace and contentment. He doesn't have the anxiety, unhappiness or cravings that he witnessed in the West because his life is harmonious and satisfying. That is what practising self-love really means – and we can choose that for ourselves, too.

The stark truth of Kenting Tai Situpa sat strangely uncomfortably with me, like the feeling I get when my bath goes cold and the water from the tap is no longer hot. I saw that what he was saying was true. That here in the West we don't naturally love ourselves, instead we push and punish ourselves, struggling on in jobs and situations that only drain our energy and bring frustration. Why?

Self-love is a daily practice that you can build over time. It takes time and patience to reflect deep within on what creates joy for us and what disturbs our balance or natural peacefulness. We have to recognise that we are on a journey of discovery and growth, noticing when we are punishing ourselves with unforgiving thoughts instead of enjoying that journey. Then we can make positive, healthy changes in our lives.

I Look After Me For You

Do you look after you? Are you first in the line when it comes to nurturing yourself, loving yourself, building on the foundations of health that we need? Or are you at the bottom of the pile behind family, friends, work deadlines, house chores, caring for parents or loved ones?

I used to place myself nicely at the bottom of the pile when I juggled my life. Me looking after me first felt selfish, indulgent, and irresponsible. The hard first step towards self-love for me was to STOP and think of me. To reflect on the inner me. I couldn't change the things outside of myself because I simply didn't control them. I couldn't control or change the sunshine, the seasons, the wind, the rain, like I couldn't control the feelings of the people around me, the economy, the interest rates, the house prices, the news, my clients, my friends – the list went on.

I needed to look after ME for YOU (with "you" referring to my family and friends).

ME requires a steady and solid foundation. My health, my attitude, my attitude, my words, my time usage, my language, my skills, my growth, the things that made me learn and grow, the way I talk to the inner me. I had to dig deep, discover and nurture my own inner mini UNIVERSE.

Recently a friend asked me what I meant by the word "nurture". For me, it means to pre-empt needs before you have them. Not just after shit happens. To record, list and consider what you need before you need it. Nurturing your physical, emotional, educational growth to create a supportive environment helps me to thrive and reach my potential.

It means to explore my human spirit and discover an innate wisdom in my body to overcome my illness. To follow my intuition, to find a new spirituality and awareness, to research what diet would help me thrive. I worked hard to increase positive emotions and focused on laughter, joy and future possibilities. I embraced support/my tribe with a new vigour and fed my mind by learning new life skills and maintaining my values.

These days I don't wait for change to happen to me; I jump into change with both feet and nurture myself daily to ensure I'm fighting fit. If I don't look after ME then how can I possibly look after YOU?

I'm My Own Lifeboat (supporting yourself in life's rough oceans)

It's tough some days not to let circumstances weigh you down. Don't let that happen to you. I have a friend who avoided me for a while. She didn't mean to, she loved me, I know she did because I know her well. I was sick. The cancer had been diagnosed and it had hit me hard. But I understood. When we finally spoke weeks later, she said she'd understand if I no longer wanted to be her friend. She had been through a hard time herself and had needed time.

I told her, "I don't need you to be my lifeboat, I don't need saving." I don't need my friends to hold me up out of the water. I am responsible for me. I take the time daily to build my inner strength. I take time for me.

I researched and read books on how to calm my mind, feed my mind, help me through cancer, stop me having panic attacks. (I've got a massive list of books I'd like to share with you.) I meditated and listened to anxiety audio apps (night after night my husband would walk into our bedroom and find me listening to chants, soft talking and gentle music). I created and repeated hourly affirmations such as "I'm going to live to be 90" or "I'm going to get strong". These calmed the buzzing bees in my head. Bit by bit I set up a gym in my mind and created room for a seven-step health blueprint.

But it took hours, days, weeks to do it. The reward was I grew stronger, more educated around myself, my mind, and my body. I don't need friends to be my lifeboats. Perhaps when I was younger I did, but today I sail the boat on my own and welcome my friends and family on board with open arms. I'm very far from being alone.

Meet Jill (invite your inner critic for tea)

We all have our doubts, fears, and worries. Mine grew so enormous that I spent a lot of time pushing them into a box and sitting on them. I tried to squash them down and deprive them of air, space or time to talk. But it didn't mean they went away. When I was tired or not vigilant they had a way of coming out of the box and shouting in my face. They panicked me because they were shouting out my biggest fears and worries.

One of my inner critics is a lady called Jill (yes, I've named her). She whispers in my ear that I'm killing myself every time I eat sugar or have an alcoholic drink. She tells me that one day my cancer will come back and kill me because of the unhealthy things I'm putting into my body. She shows me a film of my funeral and my children crying over my grave. She shows me a hospital bed, where I'm laying with no hair. She has no wisdom beyond mine, yet on some days her voice is louder than mine, and, if I let her, she cripples me.

So, I decided one day to close my eyes and visualise her, to let her out of the box and invite her for tea at my imaginary table. At that table, she is allowed to talk and have her say. I listen and take notes, acknowledge her voice and concerns. I feel grateful that I invited her for tea and gave her a voice. To acknowledge her concerns, to feel her presence with awareness. She has some good advice, especially about diet and alcohol; she delves deep and is in part some of my intuition. At the end of the dinner, I hug her, I thank her, and she leaves with a wave.

What Jill is saying isn't my destiny or my future, she is an inner critic only in my head. She leaves the table happy as she's had a voice and has been listened to. She has no truth or wisdom beyond mine, I'm aware, but I make sure I put her worries to one side so that I can find my peace till the next time I invite her to tea.

Try inviting your own Jill to tea one day.

Panic (Jills voice in your mind)	Power (your true voice)
I can't Why me Poor me	I can I will I am

Self-love thinking

How do you talk to yourself and how can you change this from panic to power?

The Mountain Climb

My friend had asked me to climb Mount Toubkal, north Africa's highest mountain at 4167 metres. Neither of us had ever climbed a mountain before. With my fear of heights, it felt like a crazy idea. I was also waiting for scan results to check the cancer hadn't spread to my lungs and the fear was threatening to overwhelm me. But something inside me wanted to move forward in life. To find new adventure. I longed for my wild side to come out and that need and hunger drove me to say yes.

We had set off early one morning when it was dark and cold. The ice clung to the mountainside, making the walk slippery and precarious. The fear I felt worrying about slipping off that mountain was like nothing I'd experienced since I had been diagnosed with cancer. It followed me like a shadow. I was sure I was going to fall and die at any moment. Every step I took going up made me worry intensely about the journey back down. My fear was so great, I had to grapple with it just to keep moving forward. Step by step, metre by metre, I climbed. At one stage I had to chant to myself *"One step at a time, one step at a time"* and every time I looked up the people at the top were still just tiny pin pricks on the horizon.

After many hours, when I reached the peak, I cried tears of relief. I looked over the clouds and thanked my body for its effort and for taking me on that journey. Looking over the vastness of the world from the top of that mountain bought about a calmness and perspective I'd not had for months. In that moment I felt with all my mind and soul that I was well and that no cancer existed in my body. I loved my body for being strong, reliable, and healthy enough to carry me up the mountain.

I trusted myself and my inner voice and all the energy I'd put into nurturing my body and soul had been worth it.

When eventually we retraced our steps, the sun was out, all the ice had melted, and we had no problem with the descent. It showed me again that living in fear of the future is pointless. Future problems are much worse in your imagination than in reality. Do not let fear of what *might* happen destroy the happiness of the present moment. As the stoic philosopher Lucius Seneca says, "We suffer more in imagination than in reality". One of the most powerful stoic exercises to combat this is the "worst-case scenario" exercise, which forces our perception of a future event to match reality, thereby allowing us to get rid of the fear associated with that event.

For example, 17 years ago I had a period of time at work that I didn't enjoy after returning from having my son. I felt as a woman that my career had been written off. I couldn't see a path forward and no one was showing me the way. I'd had a baby, not a brain transplant, and I was still super ambitious.

My nature growth mindset was jumping up and down waiting to be heard.

I feared leaving my job because I worried about the possibility of becoming homeless and starving to death (okay, it might sound irrational, but our minds can sometimes run wild). So, I took the time to vividly imagine the worst-case scenario of resigning. In my imagination, I handed in my notice, left the office, took the tube ride back home, and fetched a drink from the fridge. But then, a realisation struck me. I still had enough money to take the tube home and buy a drink? That day, nothing else had changed in my life except for the fact that I no longer worked for that specific company. The actual fear I held wasn't really about finding another job; it was more about the apprehension of feeling trapped, lacking opportunities for advancement or personal growth. Believing in and loving myself, as well as my ability to change and adapt.

I addressed that fear right away by updating my LinkedIn profile, deciding what training might freshen up my abilities, got more active online and planted a seed in my mind that maybe I set up my own company (which I later did). In other words, I just shifted my perception about fear of leaving my job into an exercise of focusing on things I could control. As Will Smith told his son in the movie *After Earth* that I watched last week, *"Fear is not real. The only place that fear can exist is in our thoughts of the future. It is a product of our imagination, causing us to fear things that do not at present and may not ever exist. That is near insanity. Do not misunderstand me danger is very real but fear is a choice."*

In my coaching, I guide individuals to initiate self-love and self-belief by effectively managing and comprehending their fears. How they perceive events in their life and what they choose to focus on causes them to suffer more (and longer!) than the actual event itself. If they really hate their jobs or are destined to lose a job, I encourage them to move through the pain of the moment when it actually happens and then let it go. To examine the opportunities for growth by making a change and imagining the feeling of bouncing out of bed keen to get into work.

One Human Soul to Another (to love is to listen)

Whether I am coaching senior executives or a client who lives in my road, I approach things from the same direction. We are just two human beings, one talking to another. By digging deeper and breaking down the barriers, the wealth, age, race and gender gaps melt away. In every session there is an underlining issue – this person simply wants to be heard. They want to be listened to, to be considered for that moment in time, with attention, focus and care. Listening is a gift you can give to someone for free. And it makes them feel valued.

My mom's saying, 'That's why God gave us one mouth and two ears,' always makes me smile. Listening to someone stops you assuming you know what they want and what is good for them. Listening turns every conversation into fascination and curiosity over what a person wants, what their hopes are for the future, where they want to head and what they want to be remembered for.

Self-Love Equals Self Belief

"They will never work with us," my new business colleague said to me one day when I added a large global brand to our client wish list.

"Why not?" I asked.

"Because, they have thousands of companies already working with them that offer similar to what we do. We would be lucky to get them to ever consider us," she said.

I reflected on this answer. My first thought was, she's right, why would this company ever work with us/me. I'd spent thousands of moments wondering if we had it in us as a business to keep growing, to keep attracting new clients, to keep paying the bills. That fear at time was overwhelming and grew with our ever-increasing responsibilities. My self-belief wavered in seconds from feeling like I was a superhero to a useless human being.

Our company was still smallish, we had 40 people and were just based in London. I had put together a list of companies I wanted us to work with, companies that would hopefully want to work with us. The brand I'd added to this list was leading in sustainability, culture, the FTSE top 100, and I really wanted to work with them and help with their growth and aspirations.

As my colleague started to remove the company from the list I suddenly blurted out, “But why would they not believe that they would be lucky to work with us?” In that moment, I really believed in myself, in my team, in our passion, our creativity, our energy and our drive. There were a thousand days when I had doubted this but that day, I felt the burning light in my soul that we would work with them. An instinct, a hunch, a moment of pure self-belief.

Six months later, I entered the global headquarters of this massive company and took a seat across from their global VP of design. Our conversation spanned 40 minutes, delving into topics such as sustainability, the future of the planet, philosophical concepts, life, creativity, and the potency of ideas. It was an encounter of shared intellect and spirits, and 18 years down the line, we remain steadfast friends. His influence on me is multifaceted and enduring. He's since confided, "You were the first person from an agency to leave our boardroom without soliciting work." Not even a day after that meeting, he had dispatched a brief to us. I collaborated with him over numerous years, engaging in various projects and providing him with insights, ideas, and my energy. I'm immensely grateful that I held onto my belief!

NOW TAKE ACTION!

Keep these 10 truths close to your heart

1/ Love is the solution; fear is the problem.
2/ Love operates on a higher universal frequency than LOVE TO FEAR.
3/ Love heals and creates new possibilities.
4/ Awareness of self-talk, self-gifts and self-belief is the beginning of self-love.
5/ Your words hold significance; they emit an energetic charge into the universe, hence, select them with discernment. Cultivate self-belief and self-love, just as Situ recommended, by repeating, "I love myself."
6/ You have to look after yourself so you can look after others.
7/ You are your own lifeboat. Invite on board people who love and light you up.
8/ Once you have made friends with your inner critic Jill, she will become one of your valuable friend.
9/ Fear of tomorrow is always greater than the reality.
10/ You can achieve the impossible through self-love and ultimately self-belief.

STEP 3: Learn and Grow

The opposite of being fearful and dissatisfied is to learn and grow. Take that course, read that book, watch that documentary, research lifehacks, and reach out to an expert in subjects you are interested in. Develop a Learn + Grow mindset – whether that is external learning about the world or internal learning about yourself.

During our younger years in education we have no choice, we must learn and grow. We might study for A levels, embark on apprentiships, take on work placements or head off to university. We then venture into the workplace and at times just stop growing. If you are lucky, you may find yourself working for a company that offers amazing training schemes – but often private industry relies on the individual to continue their learning.

If you have been in an industry or sector for decades, you can start to fear failure and change. You can get trapped by responsibility and lack of self-belief – and these things stop you growing. Or perhaps you've become a leader, an expert in your field, and you don't want to just retire and stop learning. Even into your most senior years, your brain wants to grow.

I'm so proud of my dad. After years of working as an accountant, then as an officer in the Salvation Army and finally as a head teacher in an inner-city school, he is at the age of 75 still following his passion and realising his dreams. He had his second painting exhibition last week at a London gallery. He's been retired for 15 years but he still has three jobs (although he doesn't perceive them as work). He steers a head teacher's forum, he's treasurer of an art society and secretary of a famous art institution. He's as active and growing as he was in his 20s and because of this his mind is sharp and his body is healthy. He spends lots of time still gardening, playing golf, and visiting his grandkids – what an inspiration!

Stop Pulling The Quilt Over Your Head

Life is overwhelming, complicated, ever changing and there are days for us all when we want to hide under the duvet. When animals are afraid, they hide in the long grass and wait to feel safe. But like that animal, we long to feel the wind on our face, to race across the fields, to nurture our young and to play. We need to move forward. As much as you want to, you can't hide in the grass for long.

When I feel upset and need comfort I lay on the grass or feel leaves in my hands. I run across my wet lawn and let my bare feet touch the ground. There are always obstacles in our way, things that make us sad and despair, but this is life. Let your authentic self-come run free…follow your intended path.

Learning and growing helps you to tap into and release your inner power and inner guru. Sometimes we need a map to show us where we need to go, other times we have to follow our instinct. Understand what lights you up and really start to believe that there are opportunities for growth out there in the world for you – the universe is an infinite thing and there is enough for us all.

Draw upon your past memories and experiences, but avoid replaying them incessantly. Use them as lessons rather than drowning in them. Grant yourself the space to reflect upon them, mourn any losses, acknowledge your emotions, and progress toward enhanced regulation. However, avoid pressuring yourself. Exercise patience and traverse this phase with a spirit of learning, akin to a newborn taking its initial steps in a world of awe. Embrace emotions openly, maintain curiosity toward new experiences, remain present in the current moment, and craft a potent vision for your future. Set boundaries with people and allocate time for yourself – this will foster healthier connections and provide a sense of security, worth, and comfort.

What are you doing different today that will make a difference to tomorrow? Start to sow the seeds of a new you. Personal learning and growing brings a sense that you are in control of your life. It enables you to make positive decisions, and to take action that will bring you closer to achieving your goals and ambitions.

Learning to Aid Good Health and Happiness

We need to keep learning and growing and not be afraid of using tools such as ChatGPT, the chatbot developed with artificial intelligence. We need to harness technology for the greater good and not lose our curiosity for life. As humans, we always have new things, ideas and innovations to add to society so we need to stay connected to our natural intuition to develop.

In his book "Future Shock," US author Alvin Toffler wrote, "The illiterate of the 21st Century will not be those who cannot read and write, but those who cannot learn and relearn."

We can lament the continuous stream of meetings and deadlines, or we can harness new technology to complement us, liberate our time, and foster a more harmonious life-work balance. In reality, technology can liberate us from the mundane and propel us into realms of greater creative thinking and imagination. It compels us to introspect, scrutinize our relationship with the planet, and contemplate our survival upon it. The book by Mo Gawdat,"Smart scary" is a must read to understand this new world. For individuals like me with dyslexia, it can be a transformative force.

An Accidental Entrepreneur

"Have patience with all things, but chiefly, have patience with yourself. Do not lose courage by considering your own imperfections, but instantly set about remedying them: every day, begin the task anew."

– Saint Francis de Sales

Many people I coach tell me same thing about their experiences. They didn't dream of owning their own business – they just didn't feel like they were learning and growing in the right environment and had to make a change. They had to add more ingredients to their life in order to nurture their own growth.

I didn't start in the kitchen with a few jars, some petals and a natural set of ingredients ready to make face creams. I am an ideas person with an insatiable and curious mindset. Some days I have millions of bright ideas and others just a few sluggish ones. At times I read till my mind pops with information! The thing about being in the business of ideas is that tomorrow there will always be a better one. People will always want new and more relevant things. Every day change comes upon us and how we embrace it is our choice. We must not only expect change but accept it. Change is inevitable.

I became an accidental entrepreneur because being a women and a company director and a mom with a career was difficult. I decided to set up my own business with a friend and do it my way (or our way). My two businesses have been built on helping clients with their unmet need to grow their business, brands, people and ideas.

Since then, my life has been brimming with global travel and client meetings. I've collaborated with some of the world's largest brands, and for the most part, it's been an enjoyable journey. Yet, akin to constructing a sandcastle, there have been days that felt playful and fun, but I'm aware that my achievements might wash away when the tide rolls in. My inner voice would often whisper that it's all futile, that I'm inadequate, and question the purpose amidst the relentless waves of change. Nevertheless, each day I recommence, discover new clients, and embark on fresh adventures.

I choose to adapt to change, to grow and focus on the learning and embrace that being an entrepreneur perhaps wasn't quite so accidental after all. It was simply me intuitively recognising what I wanted in life, diving in and going for it. This is living; this is life.

Understand and Defining Your Growth Values

We all have that feeling at times when we want to run away in order to find ourselves. When you are under a lot of pressure, you feel like out of control. You have no direction in life. You don't know what you are doing or why you are doing it. You begin to question the importance of your own desires and decisions. What you are looking for is to find your true values, your identity, the thing that we perceive and understand as "our true passionate self".

Living by your personal values sounds easy. Your values are your personal guide rails, so it should be natural to live by them. Sometimes when I'm not living by my values, I feel uncomfortable or upset and without direction. Have you ever been in one of these situations in life? Someone said or did something that you strongly disagreed with, but you didn't speak up about it and felt ashamed afterwards. You set a goal or aim for yourself and didn't make it happen. What you want often clashes with what you've got to do or what's practical. You're so busy pleasing other people that you're not even sure what your own true values are.

Does this resonate with you?

Values matter because you're likely to feel better if you're living according to your beliefs and worse if you don't. This applies both to day-to-day decisions and to larger life choices. If you define your personal values, prioritise them and live by them so that your actions align with your values, then you will start to feel better about yourself and more focused on what you want to achieve. Brands invest millions in defining their values. I know this well; I've collaborated with some outstanding ones to shape these pivotal elements.

Why are brand values important? They help a business attract new customers, build brand affinity and loyalty, attract and retain employees, improve business operations, and stand out from the competition. So why don't we spend the time defining our own values? When you understand your own values, you can make decisions confidently, knowing that you have your own back. Once you understand what your values are, you can use them to help set goals and make plans.

Let's begin with a reminder of what personal values entail and their significance. Personal values encompass the principles that hold importance for us – the traits and conduct that inspire us and direct our choices. When encountering individuals who do not share these values, it can result in conflict, disillusionment, and lingering dissatisfaction.

Everybody is different, and what makes one person happy may leave another person feeling anxious or disengaged. Defining your personal values and then living by them can help you to feel more fulfilled and to make choices that make *you* happy, even if they don't make sense to other people at first.

For example, maybe you value honesty. You believe in being honest wherever possible and you think it's important to say what you really think. When you don't speak your mind, you probably feel disappointed in yourself. Or maybe you value kindness. You jump at the chance to help other people, and you're generous in giving your time and resources to worthy causes or to friends and family. If your value is being wild or adventurous, you'll probably feel stifled if you let yourself be pressured by others into making "safe" choices, such as a stable office job and a settled home life. For you, a career that involves travel, starting your own business, or other opportunities for risk and adventure, may be more appropriate.

Thinking about what makes you feel good is an excellent place to start. Someone who values honesty will feel good when they tell and speak the truth. That same person will feel bad about themselves when they are not being honest. Your negative emotions can be an alarm bell, signifying that you are not being your authentic self. Acknowledge these moments promptly – it can prevent complications in the future.

What's important to you in life? What type of news story inspires you or makes you angry? When have you felt disappointed in yourself? When were you most proud of yourself? When were you the happiest? In some cases, the values will be easy to figure out. If you wrote "a loving relationship" in response to the question about what's important to you, then "love" is an important personal value for you. If you wrote "being happy", then you value happiness.

If you're inspired by stories of entrepreneurs, maybe you value determination or achievement, or maybe it's wealth and success. I often find myself reading lots about new business ventures and sometimes feel like I need to be more driven.

If you're inspired by helpers trying to change the world, maybe you value courage or integrity, or maybe it's justice or peace. As a cancer survivor, I read for a year about organisations helping people with cancer, which drove me to work with Future Dreams, a cancer charity. Doing this activated my "kindness" and "integrity" values.

Try to draw up your own list of personal values. When you've finished brainstorming, you may have half a dozen values, or you may have a list of dozens. If you're in the second camp, try to cut the list down to something manageable – perhaps 10 values that mean the most to you. If you're struggling, try assigning scores to each one and then sorting the list into an order.

Once you've compiled your list, it's essential to prioritise your values to further refine what truly matters to you. If you hold curiosity, honesty, health, kindness, adventure, and a handful of other qualities dear, the lack of distinct hierarchy might lead to ambiguity. However, if you place "health" at the pinnacle of your list, you'll recognise that developing a daily exercise regimen and making dietary improvements should assume priority. Should "adventure" occupy the top spot, perhaps planning that journey to the Galapagos Islands will take precedence. Ideally, of course, you'll aspire to live in alignment with all the values on your list. Yet, your time and energy are finite. Prioritisation enables you to concentrate predominantly on aspects that will contribute most significantly to your life.

With your list of values in hand, take a moment to consider if your life is in harmony with them. Does your career choice resonate with your values? What about your activities beyond work? Are you investing your time in endeavors that genuinely matter to you?

When I'm off track, I know it in my gut and it's usually because I'm not practising my values daily. When I work with businesses defining their values, I ask them to make a list of things they could do to put those values into practice. I'd like you to do the same.

Let's say you've chosen "learning" as a value. In that case, you could consider returning to college to finally pursue that dream degree. Alternatively, you might commit to reading a book every week on a subject that resonates with you.

Exploring online training courses or enrolling in classes at your local adult education centre are also viable options. The opportunities are abundant.

Write a long list of possible actions for each value and do something about achieving them. It doesn't have to be a massive goal either – living to your values in your day-to-day life is just as important. Make a habit of reading your list every day and whenever you find yourself straying, ask yourself what you could have done differently.

Core values to reflect on – which ones feels right?

Accountability, Adaptability, Altruism, Appreciation, Authenticity, Acceptance, Benevolence, Balance, Compassion, Caring, Collaboration, Communication, Courage, Curiosity, Determination, Empathy, Empowerment, Equality, Fairness, Flexibility, Generosity, Gratitude, Humility, Harmony, Innovation, Inclusivity, Integrity, Justice, Kindness, Loyalty, Nurturing, Open-mindedness, Optimism, Patience, Positivity, Personal Growth, Respect, Responsibility, Resilience, Self-discipline, Sustainability, Teamwork, Tolerance, Trust, Unity, Valour, Vision, Wisdom.

Learning is About Understanding the inner YOU

One of the joyful things I learnt from building brands and businesses was how to develop personality boards. These are a type of moodboard, showing images of the character the company would want to be if they were a person and not a brand. How would that brand look, think and speak? This is also a handy trick if you want to build a social media profile – how do you want to look to the outside world and differentiate yourself from others?

Certain social media moodboards can be misleading and not at all aligned with the person's own values. You might ask, who really cares? Well, in the online world, everyone cares and observes how you portray yourself to the world. I'm not here to pass judgment, but I do encourage you to be authentic and stay true to who you are, as this approach helps avoid complications.

Intuitive thinking

Build a personality board – a mood board with images of what you want to BE.

Focus on creating the lifestyle you want for the inner/outer you: how you want to look + feel, think + act, speak + sound.

Aims:

- To think about what you need externally to help you to learn and grow.
- To learn more about the inner YOU and your eco-system/inner universe. What do you need inside of you to help you grow.
- To define your values, your purpose, how you look, think, and speak in the world.
- What do your inner (your fire/energy) and outer resources (financial, network) need to look like to support you?

Power Up Your Skills

In my late 40s, I felt the need to add other things to my toolbox. I think it was because I felt like I'd exhausted the learning I could do in my sector and I wanted to retrain and grow. So, I did three courses that helped to change my life: a creative writing course at Curtis Brown, an executive coaching course at Henley Business School and an innovation online course at Harvard University. Writing, coaching, innovation – what's the link? There wasn't one! These were just the three areas I felt I was gifted in, enjoyed doing and lit me up. I was hoping they would be dots that I could join up in the future and already they are just that. Many of the things that I learnt are helping me to write this book.

It's difficult to tell you why I wanted to study at Harvard University. My natural bent towards creativity was a far leap from its business school but it was a seat of learning that I had always dreamt of joining. I wanted to superpower my growth.

The university offered an online course, exposing students to global business leaders from brands such as IBM, Philips and T-Mobile. I jumped in and signed up to a six-week course in "innovation thinking". My 40 fellow students were from all over the world and from many industries. We connected and soon became a thriving online community, sharing our observations and feedback. I even had the opportunity for a one-on-one connection with a director from Google, who generously provided me with advice regarding funding for a not-for-profit project that I plan to pursue in the future. At the end of the course, not only had I developed my understanding around innovation, but I'd broadened my mind and had my view of the world challenged.

On my coaching course, I chatted to a woman who was concerned that after having had a successful banking career, she would now be pigeonholed as a coach. It made me realise that none of these things need define us. Learning new skills simply adds tools to your kit. With these tools I felt refreshed, reinvigorated, and ready to kick off the next chapter of my life. My next course is in sustainable business modelling as the world needs help in this direction!

Opportunities for Growth

"Had I the heavens' embroidered cloths,
Enwrought with golden and silver light,
The blue and the dim and the dark cloths
Of night and light and the half-light,
I would spread the cloths under your feet:
But I, being poor, have only my dreams;
I have spread my dreams under your feet;
Tread softly because you tread on my dreams"

– *He Wishes For The Cloths of Heaven, WB Yeats*

Michelangelo said, "The greater danger is not that our dreams are too lofty and we fail to achieve them but they are too small and we do." Most of us are too afraid to dream big because as soon as we do it creates a large crevasse between where we are and where we'd like to be. Are your values and personality boards aligning with your future dreams?

Allow yourself to dream about what you want in the future and then start tapping into your inner magic to make it happen. Ask yourself, "Is everything I'm doing taking me where I want to go every day, every week, every year?" Just crossing your fingers and hoping that you are heading in the right direction, is not enough. You need to take charge. Direction determines destination. I've learnt that if you don't make plans of your own, you will fit into someone else's plan. Doing less than you can also messes with the mind. Imagine doing a little less every day – how would that look in 5 years' time? It would ruin your life! Do a little more each day, and soon new things will happen.

I've heard it said that cancer is the "wisdom disease", which is a more polite way of saying it usually happens to older people. The truth is, cancer affects children and young adults too and a diagnosis can be the kick up the bum to reflect on your future. At 39 I had this insight and it changed my core being. It made me realise that life is short and put me on alert. Cancer created a new wisdom that made me stop, reflect and dream big! I'm still dreaming today and won't ever give up on that, but I will also make sure I action things straight away so that I make the most of this one life I have.

An exercise to help you learn and grow

Ask yourself a few questions:

Is this the direction I want for my life?

Have I had a goal that's been ingrained since childhood?

Is the goal mine?

What five things have I accomplished that I am proud of?

Take a piece of paper and write on it the following:

WHAT AM I GREAT AT?

WHAT DOES THE WORLD NEED?

WHAT DO I LOVE?

WHAT CAN I BE PAID FOR?

The SWEET SPOT In the middle creates a mission for you to aim for

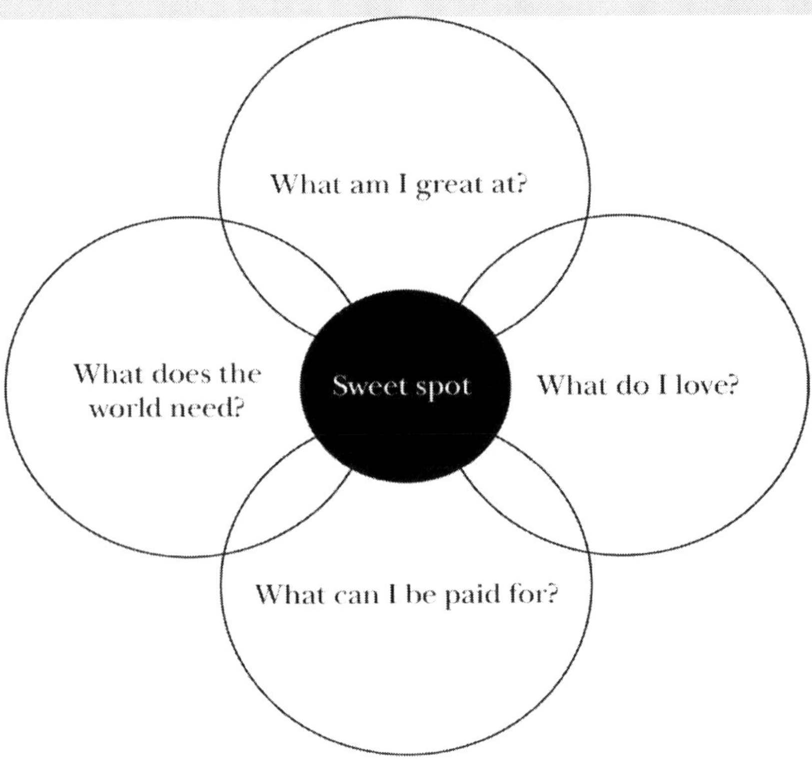

An example from me:

WHAT AM I GREAT AT?

I have learnt to be an unshakable optimist, resilient and quick thinking – reinventing and pivoting to adapt to life's changes and challenges

WHAT DOES THE WORLD NEED?

Less fear and more action

WHAT DO I LOVE?

Working with people to give them the power to unlock their potential, turning ideas into action

WHAT CAN I BE PAID FOR?

Coaching and writing

MY MISSION:

I am on a journey to help people become more powerful in the face of fear and to lead change in their lives. To take decisive action, so that together we can help our world have a more sustainable future.

Building your Legacy

"If you don't *stand for something, you'll fall for anything"*

– Alexander Hamilton

My 85-year-old neighbour texted me at work to let me know my eldest son was sitting in her lounge. He'd left his key at school and my husband had popped out. Days later he told me the story of his hour with her and admitted the effect it had on him was profound. She had shown him her photo album, the pages lovingly worn. Each photo revealed another glimpse into her life – as a child with her parents, at her wedding with her proud husband, as a new mum holding a baby, years later with four young children, the children growing older. As she turned each page, she smiled more. At 85 she'd lived almost the whole of her life in that house, she'd walked round the local parks with her babies in prams, she'd had a wonderful marriage until losing her husband to bowel cancer 15 years earlier. Her four children had each had two children and one was heading, much to her delight, to Oxford university. "A clever clogs," she beamed. My teenage son had been captivated. *"There she sat alone, Mum. In that huge empty house smiling at the memories of her life captured in time by each photo, super proud of her legacy."*

An exercise to help you learn and grow

Look forward 20 years and imagine yourself looking at your own photo album. What memories would you like to have? How would you want people to think of you at your funeral? Build a real-life photo album of yourself and your loved ones to look back on.

Where Attention Goes the Energy Flows (control the controllable)

"And as you realise that no-one outside of yourself can actually control how you feel you can start to incorporate this thinking into your daily life and develop it as a thought habit."

— Dr P.P. Surana, *'Gandhi: The Eternal Management Guru'*

Why do we spend so much time worrying about things you have we have no power over? None of us can control or change the sunshine, the seasons, the wind, the rain, the feelings of the people around us, the economy, interest rates, our house prices. We can prepare for potential problems with insurance policies or pots of emergency money, but worrying about these things is a waste of energy if we cannot know the future.

Have you ever come across the "Circle of Concern" exercise? It's a tool that distinguishes between the things within your control and those outside of it. This concept is remarkably impactful, offering a sense of optimism and ultimately empowering you over the controllable aspects. It aids in gaining perspective. Take a moment to reflect on the aspects in your life that you CAN and CANNOT control.

The things we can control, influence or change:

- ✓ My thoughts
- ✓ My passions
- ✓ My actions
- ✓ My happiness
- ✓ My emotions
- ✓ My direction
- ✓ My mindset

There are also things I cannot control:

- ✗ What other people think of me
- ✗ Other people's thoughts and beliefs
- ✗ Other people's fear and deep emotions
- ✗ Other people's stories
- ✗ Other people's happiness or sadness
- ✗ Other people's actions
- ✗ The future that has not yet been written
- ✗ The economy, the council tax, traffic jams, the weather, the PAYE system…

Learn and grow thinking…

Try drawing your own **circle of control** to understand what you can and cannot control.

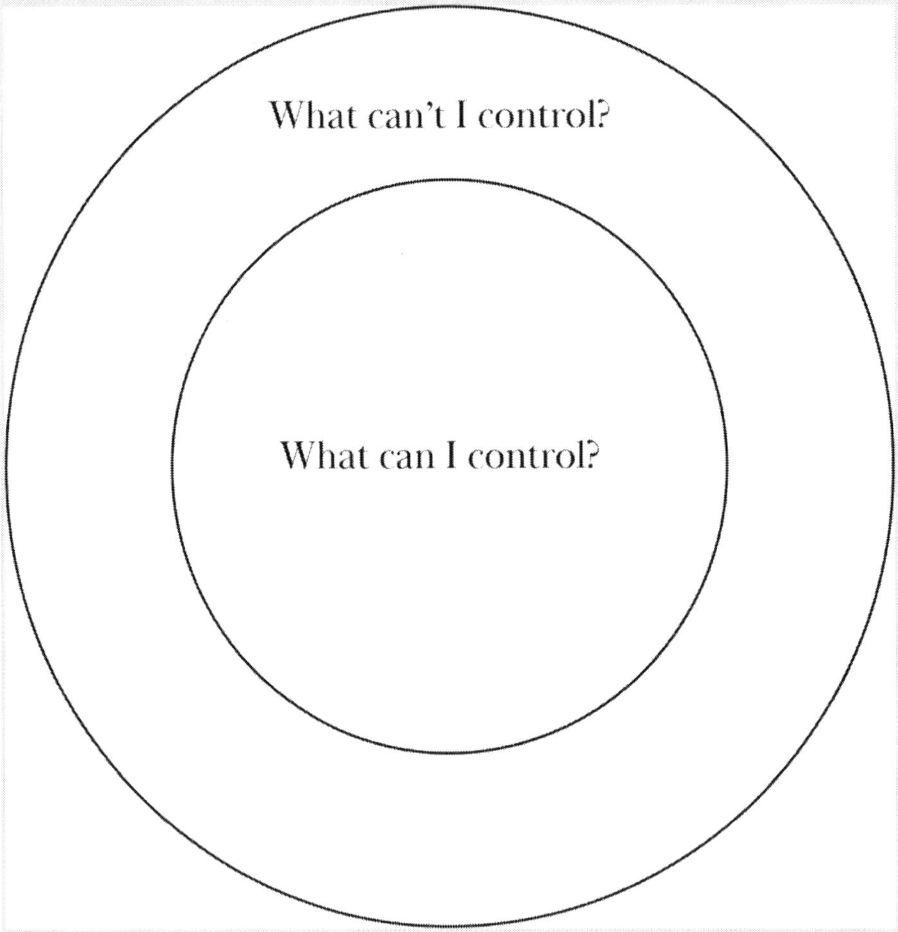

What If? (The art of possibility)

When you observe two-year-old children playing, you witness a world without limitations. Their perspective on the world and external influences doesn't hinder their imagination – anything is possible. I recently watched my friend's two-year-old engrossed in building with Lego. Curious, I inquired about her creation, half-expecting her to describe a house, plane, or wall. To my delight, she responded, "I'm making a party!" How wonderfully expansive her mind was, open to any possibility.

The "What if" exercise in life is a personal favorite of mine. It unveils the potential of boundless creativity, opportunity, and growth. I often employ this exercise in my coaching to expand my clients' thinking. I encourage them to set aside limiting beliefs and embrace a growth mindset, enabling them to discover freedom, feel lighter, and become stronger.

Just do it. Start with "What if?" What does that look like? What if anything were possible? Where would you travel, work, live? What would you do with this freedom and time?

These ideas help you find opportunities to connect or learn. What if? Anything is possible; tomorrow has not come, that thought has not been realized, so what if? Who am I, what can I become, what is my identity, where can I go? Keep repeating in your mind, "I am good, I am strong, I can do this."

Recognise that a mindset shift is needed, that if you allow it, your mind can hold you back and stop you from being your best self.

What if?

Give this a go:

What if I changed jobs, what would I dream of doing…

What if I moved house, where would I dream of living……

What if I went travelling, where would I dream of going……

What if I set up a business, what would I dream of founding….

What if I wrote a book, what would it be about?……..

What if I made a party out of lego ☺

The Blindfolded Baby (we only have one life)

On a 10-day trip to Thailand with my sister, we ventured with a local guide on a visit to an elephant sanctuary. I had given myself permission for the ultimate ME-time experience. It was my metaphorical oxygen mask going on. We snagged two affordable flights and a crazy cheap hotel on a beach. The local guide was expecting 12 people on the trip but because of the rain, there was just him and us. After a three-hour downpour, a soggy trip to the elephant park and a race round the Buddhist monument dodging the puddles, we decided to go for a beer. Our guide was hesitant at first, but we persuaded him that's what his guests wanted. After a few awkward minutes he settled down with a water in a hand and told us about his earlier life as a Buddhist monk. He spent many happy years training to be enlightened until his curiosity got the better of him and he ventured away from the ministry, married a woman and became a tour guide. Two kids later he was longing to go back to his life's calling and true purpose. I talked about my cancer and my fear of death. He listened intently and pondered and then after expressing his sympathy told us a story.

"Imagine you're a baby with a blindfold on. When you're born, you're gently placed on a towering mountain. Because of the blindfold, the ground below remains unseen. You float through the

air, descending slowly, carefree and oblivious to the concept of death. It's as if you exist without acknowledging it.

However, when illness or profound trauma strikes, contemplation about life begins. The blindfold is removed, revealing the ground beneath. Without the blindfold, the wind touches your face, and the realization of life's end comes into view. The ground approaches rapidly. This newfound understanding propels you to live life to its fullest, savoring every fleeting moment. The awareness of life's finite nature becomes evident.

Now, consider those who remain blindfolded until they crash into the ground. They navigate life without recognizing the approaching end. You, my friend, are privileged. The universe has granted you a valuable gift—the awareness of time's passage. Utilize this gift wisely. It's a chance to maximize the moments you possess, as we all inevitably meet the ground eventually."

What Would You Do If You Knew You Wouldn't Fail?

A friend of mine was starting a business and was worried about how to get it going. Then she became worried about how to keep it going, then how to stay on top of it and keep up the momentum. I told her that business – like your personal life – is like a flywheel. You need a big run up and then a massive push to get it going.

In business you need a great idea that fulfils an unmet need in the market, something that people will love and ideally need in their lives. In your own personal life, you need a goal or north star to head towards that you are passionate about.

Once you make the time to stop and think, then take that run up and push hard to get the flywheel going. Then you add in more ideas and energy and it starts to spin and build up momentum. I've seen it happen on many occasions that help will then come from unexpected places – the universe will lend a hand!

For those how don't know, a flywheel is specially designed to deliver energy, store energy and smooth out the delivery of power from the driving device (the flywheel or your idea) to a driven machine (you and your new business or personal north star).

When I'm starting to think of a new business, I start with imagining the new ideas. Then I imagine pushing the flywheel and believing in the momentum that will start to happen!!

1000 Baby Steps Towards Success

"You don't have to see the whole staircase, just the first step."

– *Martin Luther King Jr*

People have asked me over the years, "How do you get everything done?"

Most goals I've achieved have resulted because of 1000 tiny actions or 1000 baby steps, as I call them. Sometimes these steps are taken in a logical order, but mostly they are random small things I do, that I hope will work towards achieving my goal. Occasionally I come up with not just a small goal, but a big scary one. When I set myself these scary goals, they feel impossible. Like a person standing in flipflops at the bottom of an enormous mountain thinking, *"How am I ever going to get to the top*?" My fear voice always answers back first, *"Never, don't even try, you will fail and fall."* But then I calm my fear voice and take a step forward. This step can be a simple affirmation to myself, *"You can do this*" or I mention to a friend my goal and get it out into the universe. Then I have to do it.

Days later, I found I've taken five tiny steps towards this goal. I've asked a friend for advice on the subject, I've googled articles, the public affirmation turns into "You've got this". Slowly, my flipflops turn into trainers and I've walked my first 100m up the mountain with a lovely light feeling. I'm now heading somewhere with purpose.

Getting to the top is never easy, but you have to trust that the view along the way will take your breath away.

And so, when it comes to doing something that leaves a wide cavernous gap between where you are now and where you ultimately want to be, don’t think that you need to know how to bridge it before you take the first step forward.

What matters most is knowing the direction you want to head, even if you aren’t clear on a specific end-point destination. Once you know the direction, then think about what you would like to be doing 12 months from now that would be moving you towards it. Then think about what you’d be doing six months from now. Then two months from now. Then two weeks from now. Then tomorrow. Then today!

NOW TAKE ACTION!

Keep these truths close to your heart

1/ Pulling the quilt over your head stops you getting get on with life.
2/ You need to keep learning to aid good health + happiness.
3/ Embrace the enduring influence of AI-driven learning, as it continues to empower and assist individuals.
4/ You can define your personal values by reflecting on what ignites your passion. These values then serve as guiding principles for the direction you take in life.
5/ Learning also involves understanding and nurturing your inner self, not solely focusing on external experiences in life.
6/ Boosting your skills in every facet of life (wealth, health, time, social, financial) contributes to your growth and enhances your energy levels.
7/ Give yourself permission to dream and explore new ideas and "what if" possibilities; this can lead to remarkable outcomes.
8/ The energy follows where your attention is focused. Direct your attention towards activities that propel you closer to your goals
9/ By igniting the flywheel with a dynamic running jump, you set the stage for a sequence of remarkable outcomes.

10/ Rather than fixating on the daunting prospect of the 1000 steps ahead, focus on taking that initial baby step towards success.

FEARLESS WOMEN
Antonia Belcher OBE

"I divide my life into three parts. One was denying who I really was, but as a part of denying it, I, like, my only defence mechanism was to keep myself so busy that I never had time to think about it. You know, from a young age, I just neither felt like a boy nor felt like a girl, I just didn't know what the hell I was. Because when you're young, you're learning."

– Antonia Belcher OBE

Driven, self-taught, a team player and high achiever, Antonia's real gifts are her energy, resilience and an innate desire to plan. When I interviewed her for this book, she told me, "I vision what I want, see it complete and move towards it and make it happen. I can SEE the straightest line to get from A to B."

In 2022 Antonia, the founder of the Antonia & Andrea Belcher Trans Fund with Give Out, was awarded an OBE for her work for services to equality in business. Antonia's Fund provides reliable funding for activists to advocate for their communities in the places where it's hardest to be trans. To date, the Fund has raised over £100,000 to support seven trans organisations working around the world. Growing up, she locked away and kept Antonia quiet for fear of shattering her mom and dad. Enjoying construction, being great at drawings and maths, she moved to London to become a trainee surveyor in Mayfair. She worked hard to be the person that everyone wanted her to be. Her mom wanted her son to be successful, and she did her best. She grew to be a firm's partner and then a young equity partner.

For years she led a double life for years, which was very difficult for her. Then one day she decided to tell her people that she was not the person they thought she was. That there was another person hiding inside, and she needed to give that person space. It was a challenging time for her. When the time came for her to tell her five equity partners about transitioning into a woman, the thought horrified her. No woman had ever been at that level in the firm. How could she make it work? How could she stop them thinking it would be a disaster and kick her out? She had spent 20 years of her life working there; she was successful! So, she had to think of a plan when she was in this position of weakness.

Antonia created a clear plan that involved rating each partner, from the most approachable up to the least. Starting with the most approachable, she invited them each to the pub under the pretence that she had made a big mistake that could lead to the firm being sued – one of their worst fears! Before the meeting, she went home and got ready as Antonia and turned up as her true self; she then told them there was no mistake and they were not about to be sued. Each partner was so scared by the potential news of legal action that they became more accepting to listen to Antonia's story of transition.

When the company moved offices in six months, she went to work as Antonia and not Anthony, sending around an email to all the staff beforehand saying…*"Antonia is Antony, Antony is Antonia and always has been. And Antonia relishes working now. And if you've got any questions, come and speak to me, I'm happy to tell you everything. Otherwise, business as usual. And Antonia looks forward to working with you all."*

None of Antonia's colleagues came to see her, and she felt empowered and motivated to continue. Five years later, she was approached to be the next senior partner, which she turned down to set up her own business. Antonia's genius move meant she could finally be herself without prejudice; she listened to her inner voice and didn't live her life as a lie.

Antonia's joy comes from achieving things, and she's certainly amazing at doing that, having set up and sold her successful business. From 2010, Antonia embarked on her proud transgender campaign to talk about her journey and to make it clear that it was love._"Self-love and the people around you, that's the key ingredient," she told me. Being accepted by her tribe and being surrounded by people that love, accept, and care for Antonia, has been wonderful in life's journey.

"Those people who have transitioned into a solitary environment, they've got my admiration because I haven't had to do that. I've got support from my daughter, my two boys and my wife Andrea, they've been fantastic, it's wonderful. And it inspires you, that little bit of sanction that you get from the people that love you. I'm not trying to swim upstream. I've got a little bit of current going in my direction, and it's going to help me."

– Antonia Belcher OBE

Antonia's three tips for managing fear

1. **"Stand back and watch yourself":** Sometimes it looks bleak in difficult times. When things are difficult, you can make them even more difficult by dwelling on them too much. It's very easy for things to get out of control, and then you will find it difficult to create answers or solutions to deal with your issues. You need to stand back, take yourself out of the issue, and watch yourself try to become dispassionate about the issue. Emotions feed on us and play with us. You must look at facts in the cold light of day and ask yourself, what's driving that fear. Detach yourself from it and analyse it. You need to take perspective before you move forward. For example, when something is going wrong, you start thinking about the ramifications of what's gone wrong, rather than looking at why it went wrong and what you can do to undo the wrong. You start playing

out all the downstream impacts, rather than going back upstream and saying what did I do wrong, how can I make amends for it to correct the situation? Your brain wants to move the wrong way, rather than the right way, which is working out what was causing your fear.

2. **Work out what your strengths are":** Work out what good cards you have, how can you use them to your best advantage.
3. **"Create a plan. Give it weight and meaning":** Focus on an end goal, communicate with your tribe (friends, family, colleagues) clearly action the plan.

STEP 4: Find Your Joy

"In the small matters trust the mind, in the large ones the heart."

— *Sigmund Freud*

Human joy is a rich emotional state that gives feelings of happiness, contentment and pleasure. I get mine from many things. It could be from eating delicious food, spending time with my tribe (family, freinds, peers) , achieving a goal on my moodboard (yes, I do them too!) or just experiencing a spiritual or emotional moment.

I have a friend who underwent an exceedingly challenging and intricate divorce, to the extent that even the slightest glimmer of happiness brings tears of joy to his eyes. During a holiday last year, as we strolled onto the beach, I noticed him shedding tears. When I inquired, he turned to me and softly shared, "I'm just so happy." Experiencing profound sorrow has heightened his sensitivity to joy, enabling him to recognize and embrace it with his entire being—mind, body, and soul.

Joy is an essential part of our wellbeing and can help reduce our stress and anxiety, improve relationships and give a sense of purpose in life. I've spent a lot of time researching joy over the years, ever since I learnt that one of its benefits is to boost the immune system. With cancer and chemo your immune system is massively compromised so anything that makes this work better is a must for me.

But finding joy and using it to heal can be like finding a needle in a haystack. So I had to go back and look at what joy meant for me.

In my teens I discovered two things – boys and the fact that I had a constant itch. The itch was harder to handle. It wasn't one of those physical itches that was easy to scratch and forget. No, it came whenever I was drawing, cooking, writing and crafting new ideas and seemed to gnaw endlessly at my mind. The itch was the voice of my joyful gifts calling at me to be a creative. It was an absolute and unadulterated feeling of wonder and delight.

We all have joyful gifts that make us happy. As children we love that feeling but adulthood brings with it rules. We forget our joy and start working, looking after our children and building our pot of money (if we can) to provide us with choices as we get older. Along the way the joy gets lost.

Recent surveys have shown that more of us than ever before are experiencing burnout. We often feel drained, detached, overwhelmed and cynical, we procrastinate and doubt ourselves. Burnout doesn't only come from overworking, it also comes from "underworking" or underutilisation of our potential, skills and talents. Here, the symptoms may not be so obvious point as a physical burnout – more to a deeper emotional and mental feeling of being "lost" or "dead" inside.

When you are using your joyful gifts, you don't feel this, instead you soar into the sky like a bird, fulfilled and content. But we all at times forget our joyful gifts or can't remember what they are.

Identify Your Joyful Gifts (and use them)

"Don't ask yourself what the world needs; ask yourself what makes you come alive, then go do that. Because what the world needs is people who have come alive."

– Philosopher and writer, Howard Thurman

I remember once, when I was anxious, a friend asking me what I was passionate about – I could not think of a single thing. The fact was my joy was actually staring me in the face. To feel your joy, you have to be in the present, living here and now. Joy is something you can touch and feel in the moment. My joy was to read and write, but somewhere along the way the writing had stopped.

Thanks goodness I was still picking up books. I've always enjoyed reading and digesting books and sharing their contents with others. For example, when a friend is struggling with her business, I immediately start researching ideas to help her. When my parents couldn't work out a new mortgage deal, I enjoyed hunting out the latest bank offers then brainstorming them with Mom and Dad. When I use my joy, people are attracted to me and I have a positivity that radiates from within. When I focus on the joy and share it with others, it's like a magnet that attracts even more happiness. That joy affects my inner being, it makes me stand up taller, feel more confident and smile. It makes me live in the now and stops me fiddling with my phone and searching for somethings better and worrying about things I'm missing (that actually are already in the past). Finding my joy also pulls me into wanting more of it in my life and dreaming that anything is possible.

But I'd stopped writing. Why?

It's hard to imagine that I didn't write when I was younger. For me now, putting words on paper is like lying in a hot bath on a cold day. It makes me tingle with excitement. But it wasn't always like that. While doing my English A level I was pretty sure I was dyslexic. One day, we had a substitute teacher who'd been drafted in from the local grammar school and he gave me a stern talking to. The talk made me feel so rubbish and not at all creative, although I went on to get a B in my exam. After that I believed that writing was a waste of my time and although I wrote all my own work articles, I always had them checked and edited by a colleague.

After my cancer diagnosis, I needed to do a deep dive into what would give me joy and I realised the only writing I did was for work. I loved reading novels and stories, so why didn't I write them? I knew it was an area to be explored. A few years later, I wrote my novel *Colourful Creatures* and absolutely loved doing it, but when the book came back from the editor it had thousands of errors – spelling, grammar, sentences upside down and back to front. I was horrified at how rubbish I was but my husband told me I had been given the gift of creativity but not of spelling and grammar. I had to let it go and ask for help.

So, when I started this book, I was nervous – and then the universe heard me and sent me my lovely friend Christina.

She has gone through every page of this text and made it readable. Without her it would not have been written!

Don't expect to have every single gift given to you on a plate. At times you will need help to bring that joy to life, and having Christina by my side on this journey has made it a thousand times better than it would have been.

Joyful thinking

Create a **mood board** of all the things you'd love to bring into your world (a house, a new job, a new partner, a special holiday, etc.)

What does your dream future look like?

How will you get there?

Is the journey as important as the destination?

Will the road be paved with gold and lined with fruit trees?

What might a joy-filled future version of YOU look like?

DREAM BIG and be specific.

When will you achieve this?

Where and what will it look like?

Losing Your Joy (and finding it again)

There have been periods in my life when I have lost my way. There was a time when I was focusing on too many things that didn't delight or light me up. I spent too much time on financial planning, and not enough on creativity. I micro-managed staff because things were not happening quick enough. I argued constantly with my business partner. I felt stuck in a rut and that was when a friend asked me about my own passions and not a thing came to mind! So, I read and read and read to find an answer. I read books, online articles and magazine features. And then I waited and waited for something to happen that would give me a clue. What one thing am I passionate about, I kept thinking. Wasn't it obvious? I LOVED READING! Sometimes the things you are most passionate about really are staring you right in the face.

One day I was at the hospital for a treatment, reading a magazine article about the NHS doctors who were recommending self-help books to patients instead of automatically prescribing them anti-depressants. I looked up and noticed a man with one of my favourite books '*The Pilgrimage of Harold Fry*' (in case you haven't read the book it touches on young adult suicide with an amazing story). I asked him why he had it. He told me he was a counsellor at the local university and that he gives out a copy to every new student. Since we were both there for a long treatment, we chatted for a time about many books we each loved and recommended. Then it suddenly struck me...I must have read 1000s of books and enjoyed nearly every, single one! Why had I been wracking my brain for weeks to think what I was passionate about?

So, I loved reading books. But would ever be good enough to write one myself? I almost gave up on the idea before it was even allowed to be born. Right on cue, my fear showed up.

Who would want to read it?

"Probably nobody," said my inner critic Jill said.

Even if I do write one, who would want to publish it?

"Probably no one," came the answer from Jill. Eek!

For a long time, I dismissed the book-writing idea before it took root, just in case I failed. For months I convinced myself it was the right choice until I decided to NOT focus on the outcome but just to enjoy myself, to enjoy the process of writing. So, here I am enjoying my passion at 22:59 on a Monday night, having written non-stop for three hours, which felt like three seconds! The wind is in my sails, and I feel alive!

Joyful thinking

Take a pause and focus on yourself.

What are you passionate about?

What puts wind in your sails?

What do you do that makes time fly by?

Tip: "Bird by Bird: Some Instructions on Writing and Life" by Anne Lamott is a great book to read if you want to become a writer. I love this book. It offers valuable insights, practical advice, and a unique perspective on the writing process. Anne Lamott's approach encourages writers to take small, manageable steps and to embrace imperfection as a natural part of the creative journey. A page a day and 365 days later you have a book!

Bring on the Joy - Vision and Goal Setting

It unbelievable how complex life has become – we pack so much into our day that we sometimes feel the joy seeping out of every pore. There is so much to remember, to catch up on, to complete. It's easy to lose sight of what's important and meaningful and brings you joy. Things such as spending time with people you love or going on a much needed holiday. Urgency sucks the joy out of life. If only things were more joyful and less complex.

One of the main reasons our lives have got so joyless at times is because there is a big gap between our aspirations and what we are living on a day-to-day basis. We know in our heart if we are not living our goals. But if we haven't written them down, we might not be clear why we feel unfulfilled, what we want from our lives so that we can work towards it. If we do this, it pushes all the things that are not important to the side and lets us focus more on the joyful goals.

Be clear on your goals and visualise the life you want to lead. Make a list, chart or picture of those goals. Break the goals down into stages. Put it where you can see it every day. You cannot, as an old saying goes "eat an elephant in one go". You need to work out what your key goals are and keep working on them, making steady progress. When I achieve even the small goals on my list, I get a massive sense of achievement that makes life more joyful and easier to deal with on a day to day basis. This is your life, and you only have one shot at it, so if you're not happy with it, shake it up! Change the channel!

Here's a way that I define my goals…

1/ What do you want in the next five years – list 30 things in five minutes.

Make sure this list is not what you think you can get but what you WANT. Anything you want should be on that list (e.g. places you want to visit, experiences, jobs, a new business/adventure, changes to make/drop/drive for, people to meet, a house you want to buy, people you want to meet, investments, properties etc)

My examples:

- *Visit Thailand.*
- *Start a new coaching business.*
- *Become a published author.*
- *Earn £s to pay off the mortgage.*
- *Become a non-executive director – this came true six months after I'd set this goal.*
- *Work and raise lots of money for charity.*
- *Have a loving marriage.*
- *Buy a place by the sea.*
- *Spend more time with Mom and Dad.*

2/ Run down your list and quickly/instinctively give each item a number based on how quickly you want to achieve the goal e.g. 1 year, 2 years, 3 years, 5 years. Make sure in year one you identify three goals minimum and say WHY you want them.

Why three goals?

When the WHY is more powerful than the HOW you get there. It is so much easier to commit to. If they are strong and compelling enough goals, you will manage your time. You will be so enthused that you can get up at any hour to develop any discipline or goal.

For example: I want a new home the sea; but what is my WHY? The reason why I want it is stronger than the object e.g., the purpose for the house is a place to write – the purpose is more valuable to me than the object itself.

Some goals are personal development goals around the future person you want to become – e.g., one of my goals was to take three new courses so that I could reach a whole new marketplace with my business. it's not what you get that makes you valuable, it's what you become.

Personal development is vital, becoming a skillful, attractive person, a good partner, member of society, a contributor. The goals can also alter the course of your life. Ask yourself what type of person you want to become to achieve all you want.

What you become helps you achieve, the more you achieve the more you can become. It's a virtuous circle.

Have you dreamed of the person you want to become? Wiser, healthier, stronger? You need to build a reputation, so ask "what type of person must I become to attract the opportunities and people I need?"

3/ When you reach a goal that's important, celebrate it. Take the time to celebrate an important goal with the other people it affects. e.g. a family goal – celebrate with the family. This will encourage everyone to make a longer list (e.g., if I can accomplish that goal, then what else can I do? if I can get here so quickly, then maybe I can double this original list?)

4/ Light this fire and it won't go out. Since I was 25 no one has ever said to me "When are you going to get going". Don't get lazy, design your week, month, year, life and the favourable winds will blow your way.

Joyful thinking

Grade your wealth / health goals.

Your North Star

If you want to keep it more simple, define your north star. A "North Star" is a metaphorical term often used to describe a guiding principle or a fixed point of reference that helps individuals or organisations navigate their paths and make decisions. Just as the North Star in the sky has historically been used by sailors and travellers to find their way, a personal or professional "North Star" serves as a constant guiding light that keeps you on course even when faced with challenges or uncertainties. It represents your overarching purpose, values, and long-term aspirations, providing clarity and direction as you work towards your goals.

For example, Nelson Mandela's north star was to liberate all people from the continual bondage of apartheid in South Africa (along with injustice, poverty, violence, and other forms of discrimination). His actions day-to-day were geared towards this specific goal. Whether it was new partnership, ventures or friends, his decisions trickled down from his north star.

Can your North Star Change?

"There is no passion to be found playing small – in settling for a life that is less than the one you are capable of living."

– Nelson Mandela

Over time, you may find that your north star will evolve as you evolve. Mine did and that's fine. You may experience something that pushes you in a different direction. You may reach your goal, which means it's time to set a new target. This could mean an extension of your current goal or a new one altogether.

I believe everyone was put on this earth for a reason. Does that mean you need to solve all of the problems of the world? No. Having said that, way too many of us are stuck in "Groundhog Day", and defining your north star could be a way out of it.

So, what is your North Star?

Is it striving to be the best mother you can be?

Is it working towards reducing waste in the world?

Is it empowering individuals with cancer to live longer?

Is it embracing a life of simplicity?

Be bold in your choices, wise in your actions and brave in sharing your north star ideas with your tribe. Putting it out in the universe could be the thing you need to kickstart your journey from the kerb and onto the highway!

My north star was to become an author. Below is a diagram that I drew up with the help and perspective of a dear friend.

Joyful thinking….

Create a north star journey diagram to show how you will make progress to your destination. The example below is my north star destination, which is to become a published author by 2024. The star at the far right is reaching that goal!!

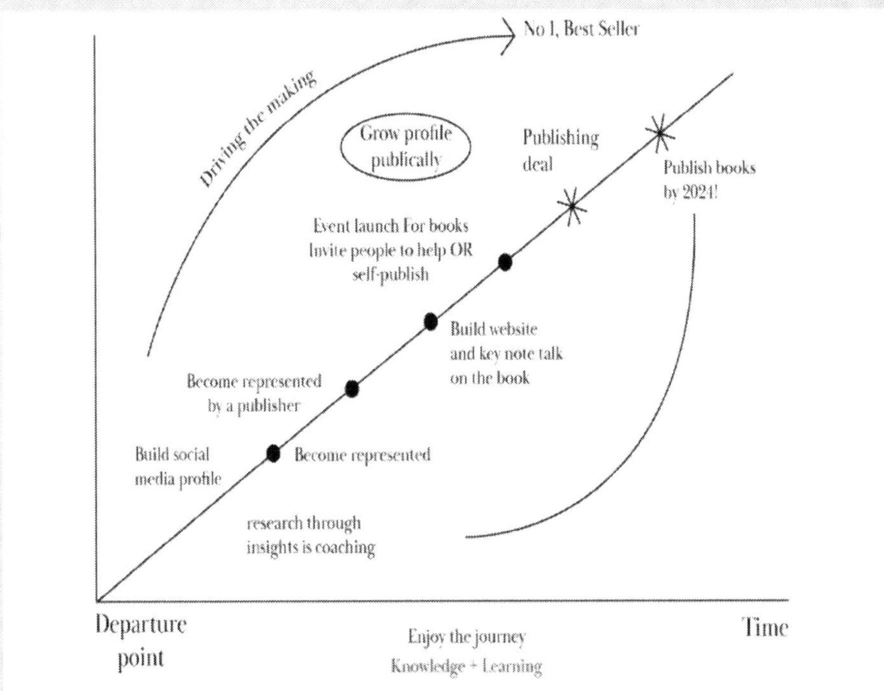

For me it has been a big, scary, difficult north star because:

1/ I'm dyslexic and need to check my spelling, punctuation and grammar.

2/ I'm not famous and don't know if people will be interested in reading my book (s).

3/ I need to work to pay my mortgage, so finding time to write is difficult

...BUT

I love writing! It lights up my soul, keeps each of my body's 30 trillion cells tingling with joy, which builds up my immune system and keeps me healthy and wealthy in mind, body *and* spirit...phew!

So, what are my steps to becoming a published author?

1/ **Dream** of the opportunity.

2/ **Desire** to do it.

3/ **Action it:** Work through the fear and distractions and keep up the momentum.

4/ Always remember it's not just about reaching the north star but about enjoying the joy and growth of the journey.

Make Your 30 Trillion Atoms Smile With Joy!

The ocean looks like a massive expanse of water but it's made up of millions of droplets of water. Similarly, our bodies comprise a harmony of trillions of atoms, each a radiant source of energy.

In moments of challenge and uncertainty – when my cancer resurfaced, my business ventures wavered, and the weight of guilt became overwhelming – I understood the necessity to turn my focus inward. I steer my attention towards my body, my thoughts, and my actions. With a determined purpose, I conjure a vivid image of the cells that reside within me, each playing a unique role in life's intricate dance.

In these moments of reflection, I gently affirm, "I am safe, I am present, I am well." It's as though my words resonate through my being, and in response, my healthy cells awaken. I imagine that they become animated with a sense of playfulness. They giggle, they jiggle, they snuggle together and care for each other, passing little hugs around.

In times of adversity, this intricate visualisation becomes a haven – a place where I connect with the essence of my existence. By invoking the joy within my cells, I kindle a transformative light that transcends the physical confines of my body. It serves as a reminder that within the complex fabric of our being lies an intrinsic potential for rejuvenation, resilience, and boundless happiness.

NOW TAKE ACTION!

Steps to help you rediscover your joy:

1.**Explore Your Joy and Gifts:** Begin by delving into your inner self to identify what brings you true joy and the unique gifts you possess.
2. **Navigate the Path:** Reconnect with the journey towards joy by reflecting on your past experiences, interests, and moments that have ignited happiness.
3. **Embrace Possibilities:** Engage in the liberating exercise of "What If?" to unleash your imagination and open doors to new horizons and unexplored potentials.
4. **Set Tangible Goals:** Translate your aspirations into actionable goals, utilising effective goal-setting techniques to give direction and purpose to your endeavors.
5. **Follow Your North Star:** Determine your guiding light, your North Star, that represents your ultimate purpose and align your actions with it.
6. **Radiate Positivity:** Cultivate positivity within yourself by envisioning your 30 trillion cells beaming with joy and creating a harmonious balance within your being.

FEARLESS WOMEN
Anna Hemmings MBE

"Sometimes it can feel like the universe is making this happen, but I think that you activate the creative subconscious. When you visualise something and bring it to life in your mind's eye, you start to activate your creative subconscious that then helps to generate ideas, creative ideas, creative ways of achieving that goal. It programs your brain to recognise and draw into your life the resources, the people, the environment that you need to make it happen."

– Anna Hemmings

After becoming a three-time kayak world champion and competing in the Olympic Games at the age of 24, Anna was diagnosed with Chronic Fatigue Syndrome (CFS), which left her feeling devoid of energy, out of sync and fearful. She went from being at her highest level in the world of sports to hitting rock bottom, which created a huge amount of fear. Before her illness, she could do 100 press-ups and chin-ups in one go. Now she couldn't even hold her hands up to wash her hair for more than 10 seconds as it was too painful.

At first, other than the permanent exhaustion and muscle pain, the doctors could find nothing wrong with Anna, which was the hardest part of her challenge, she says. Not knowing what was wrong frightened her, and it took six months before doctors diagnosed her with the condition and told her she might never race again. She felt trapped in a body that was not cooperating with an illness that she did not know how to overcome.

Eventually, her emotions and body caught up with her, and she had to stop and listen to what her body was trying to tell her. Anna realised that the emotional battle was harder than the physical one. She learnt that she was not listening to her mind and body and that charging ahead was not the answer. The turning point in Anna's life came when she discovered a treatment called the Reverse Therapy and learned the importance of expressing and opening up to the people closest to her.

Anna acknowledges the fact that she had not been good at being vulnerable and taking down the mask before her CFS diagnoses . As an athlete, she needed her game face on – to be tough, strong, and invincible. Anna realised that she could not continue to be like that off the water and outside of the competitive arena because she needed relationships and help from people around her. Anna had isolated herself from key people in her team and was not expressing her emotions and how she was feeling.

The key to Anna's recovery, she says, was allowing herself to be vulnerable, expressing her struggles and weaknesses, and being honest with herself and others, and therefore getting the support she needed. She understood that it was essential to take time for self-love and to listen to her body.

Anna's story teaches us the importance of taking time to listen to our minds and bodies and being vulnerable and honest with ourselves and others.

Amazingly, with this new inner knowledge, she fought her way back to a full recovery and won three more world titles consecutively while competing in her second Olympic Games in Beijing in 2008. Anna didn't know how she was always going to do it as no one had done it before, but in 10 months, she was back to her former self. Anna's key was taking small steps every day, one day at a time. She set her goals, visualised, and worked towards them. In 2010 Anna, who had won nine gold world and European championship medals in her career, was awarded an MBE for her services to sport.

Anna found joy using her gifts. Today, as a leadership coach and motivational speaker, she loves to help others achieve their goals and reach their potential. She has a growth mindset that is always optimistic, determined, fun-loving, and passionate about high performance and helping others succeed. Anna believes that she can help others learn and grow based on her experience. She knows that you must serve yourself before you can serve others. You cannot take on too much and should be clear about what you want and need before helping others. Anna's story teaches us that we need to take care of ourselves so that we can serve others better and the importance of building and nurturing a deep connection with yourself, your tribe, and your community.

"That is what I am most proud of, yes, I'm proud of winning, but also for the emotional battle that I had to overcome to get there. Sometimes that inner voice was helpful and sometimes it was very destructive. That inner negative voice said things like, what if you're not good enough? What if you've missed two years, you've missed too much. I had to work at replacing my inner voice with one that's more supportive and helpful."

– Anna Hemmings MBE

Anna's three tips for managing fear:

1. **"Focus on what you're great at":** This gives you confidence.
2. **"Be present":** Fear often arises when we're fixated on the future and concerned about potential negative outcomes or what might happen. In reality, most of the time, we have no control over the future, and we worry about things that might never happen.
3. **"Be aware of your thoughts":** Know they are just that – in your head. If you are giving energy to them, then they just get fuelled. And so be present enough to notice those thoughts and then separate the facts from the interpretation or the story. Reframe or replace that story with more helpful thoughts or facts.

STEP 5: Find Your Tribe

"You are the average of the five people you spend most of your time with."

- Jim Rohn (Tony Robbins teacher)

Contrary to social media misconceptions, we each have just five powerful influencers – friends and lovers that dictate our destiny. Do we choose them, or do they choose us? Get it wrong and the consequences are catastrophic.

In the past, I held the belief that happiness required surrounding oneself with joyful individuals. Yet, as time has passed, I've come to grasp a deeper truth: our accomplishments and contentment in life are intricately tied to the people who comprise our tribe – the conscious choices we make about the company we keep. This tribe can either uplift us to new heights or plunge us into the depths of negativity.

Who holds the key to your survival and growth? Have you recognised those who genuinely support you, those who fan the flames of your passions and drive? Take a closer look at everyone within your sphere, take stock of their influence. Now is the ideal moment to seek out and cultivate your tribe, to dedicate attention to nurturing your connections. Identify those who can contribute to translating your dreams into reality. Then, expand your reach to discover your broader community, network, and global role. During challenging times, I often reach out to family or friends and enquire about the reasons they value our friendship and what aspects of me they appreciate. Their responses never fail to brighten my perspective!

I've heard it said that if you want to be successful you should surround yourself with successful people. If you want to be healthy, you should surround yourself with healthy people. Supposedly it helps you become more like the people you hang out with. Now I'm not sure how true this is. The biggest lesson I've learnt is what makes a supercharged powerful tribe is one when you and the people within it complement one another.

When you are in a circle that overlaps with other people – their gifts in your life, and your gifts in their life – you can do amazing things. It's like adding all the ingredients into an enormous, amazing cake. Baking is like science. For example, I needed people with specialist skills to complete this book. So, I reached out to two people in my tribe and asked them to add in their ingredients of knowledge, grammar and creative design etc and together we produced something fabulous that, I hope, will help you to find your own perfect recipe..

Take a moment to reflect on the following: Who are the people you spend most time with? Do they elevate you or bring you down? Are they proactive go-getters exhibiting qualities that you admire or people who just sit and criticise? Do they motivate or drain you?

My Tribe

I celebrated my hen night in the best way possible. For two days I was surrounded by 19 amazing women from some of my different tribes and I felt lucky to have them. I had spent years nurturing and growing these friendships through the good times, but sadly, my hen weekend took place during a period that was challenging. I was worn out because of my cancer treatment. I was sleeping too much and felt vulnerable. It meant a lot to me to have 19 friends around me on the eve of my wedding.

I should not have been surprised. Each one of those women had been there for me during my treatment. As I went through 12 sessions of chemotherapy, my tribe united to become one powerful group. Each week one or two of them would come with me to chemo session to play games, laugh, talk, and share stories. So rather than chemo being something I dreaded, it became something I looked forward to. I was amazed when the WhatsApp group was set up and how quickly the weekly slots filled. They all wanted to help, and this was a way in which they could.

Last year the same thing happened when my husband unexpectedly had a heart attack and I suddenly found hotpot casseroles waiting on my doorstep. Despite my pride wanting me to decline the help, I knew it was exactly what I needed. Thank you for that.

My tribe is not one of life's "nice-to-haves"; it's essential to me. My tribe has kept me afloat in troubled times. Over the years my tribe has evolved, and some members even disappeared as my life required new tribe members, each vital because they created new connections and a sense of belonging. When a friend went through AA, she found she no longer had anything in common with 50% of her old tribe. The common ground had been alcohol and with this gone the connections faded. Three years later she found herself with a whole new tribe that focused on a deeper spiritual conversation that fuelled her soul. She was sad about the old tribe, but the new tribe mirrored her aspirations for the future.

It's Okay to Let Some of your Tribe Go

I once had a close friend who I'd known for years but who I felt had gradually changed over time. I wasn't sure why, but I take responsibility for my share of the problem, even though I didn't realise we had one until it was too late. It broke my heart to see her leave my life. It took years for me to truly let her go from my mind and heart. But when my cancer came it bought with it suffering and a new learning and meaning. Life became profound, deep and impermanent and all the materialist things lost their shine This friend continued to live her life with our old meaning, so our mindsets differed, our values differed, and she found a new tribe to run with. It was hard. I felt like she had died, even though she was just down the road. I was tempted so many times to make contact, but I knew that with my learnings we couldn't make each other laugh or smile or happy any more. So, she stayed in her new tribe and I learnt that sometimes friends are not forever.

You need change. People need change. So don't fight it. The best way to heal and grow is to let those friends go into their own wilderness. But even though we grew apart as friends, know this: most days I'm still cheering her on from afar and I still love her deeply.

Toxic Tribe Members

You need to do more than just exercise and eat healthy food, you need to spend time around good, positive people. They need to align with your values, your ethos, your visions. They need to cheer you on when times are tough and clap and smile when you achieve amazing things. But not everyone will fit into your tribe.

Some people will suck the joy out of your life. It could be a family member, a friend, a lover or a colleague, and the thought of not having them in your life might make you scared of the unknown. But toxic people are toxic to your health and happiness and you need to defend these things at all cost. It's a battle that must be won with respect.

Say no to people pleasing, accepting people in your life who hold you back and dim your light, but know that we are never too old to make new friends. So be open to that.

Tribes Connect You In A Common Goal

Tribal groups are about *connection.* We're born into tribes – ethnicity, religion, gender – but as adults we can *choose* the tribes we identify with and for the period in our lives that we need it. People come together through shared passions and interests. My tribe at the Future Dreams breast cancer charity is a powerful example of a group coming together to support people going through cancer. Please check them out and become part of our tribe (https://futuredreams.org.uk).

Tribes can last a lifetime or a short time, evaporating when the purpose is no longer, like my antenatal group. It worked as my most intimate community of friends while I was going through all the experiences of being a new mother. It was my security blanket. Almost 17 years later, while I am still friends with many of them, the tribe has completed its purpose.

Five years ago, one of my antenatal NCT friends was diagnosed with liver cancer and she called me in a panic saying the doctors had given up on her. We bonded all over again like we had over the birth of our children. I gave her the words of comfort we all need to hear in those dark times saying, "You are going to be ok, I can feel it, find a new medical team that have faith, find a new medical tribe." Today she is strong and living her best life. She has proven the original doctors wrong and surrounded herself with people who believe she has a future. Did I lie when I said to her, "You are going to be ok." No, I didn't. I believed that she was going to be well and that if she didn't start believing it for herself she would go downhill.

We all need to believe and we need our tribe to believe in us, too. I believe that for a healthy tribe to be effective and harmonious, each member needs to contribute, to bring their openness, receptivity, and a willingness to share, to support, to listen and connect. Each member of our tribe needs to believe in us and our future.

A healthy tribe is built on:

1. Belief
2. Trust
3. Honesty
4. Vulnerability
5. Respect
6. Authenticity
7. Love
8. Sharing of all things joyful

Some People Come Into Your tribe Just When You Need Them

Have you ever asked the universe for help? One day, in desperation, I did just that. When you have had cancer twice, despair is like turning on a blue ambulance light above your head. On that awful day, I lay on the ground under a tree in my garden and asked for something, somebody, to save me. A day later a WhatsApp message popped into my inbox inviting me for a walk and a coffee. It made me realise that some friends are for a lifetime, some for a season, and some come exactly when you need them.

I'd known the women who answered my prayers on the "outside" for a long time. Confident, visionary, pioneering, and beautiful, she was a businesswoman sitting on a global stage who was offering me her time. She was also a woman who was living with cancer, so her time was more precious than any bar of gold.

When we met, the walk was muddy, but then so was life. The coffee was cold, but then humans were easily distracted. Our conversation however, was clear and warm.

The woman on the "inside" was thoughtful and so quiet at times I wondered if she could hear me among the bird song, the mud slushing, the conversations of the other walkers and my crying. I stole a glance from time to time to see what she thought of my problem. Her face was still and calm.

I learnt on my coaching course many months later (taken because of some of the advice she gave me that day) that when you're really listening to a person, you sometimes mirror that person's anger and displays of frustration and repeat their words back to them. For example, saying, "Wow, yes, that sounds awful," isn't the most effective way of helping a person. The best gift is to deeply listen. To be calm and hold the space without a response. To give the other person time to talk without throwing logs onto their burning emotions. It's a gift to be heard and listened to without judgement, without mirroring and without prejudice.

A new soul connection was made on that walk and a bond formed from a place of deep listening. The message and advice she gave me were personal, my problem was messy, but the depth of her thought and the clarity of advice were phenomenal. We talked about how to turn things from frustration to fascination. We looked for, dreamt of, and imagined a new road for me to walk down. Her words and messages offered kindness, belief, and encouragement.

"I'm so excited I have a moodboard filled with my dreams for 2023 and the ideas we've talked about, I'd love to show you," I said one afternoon.

"Don't call them dreams," she said, smiling and did a little clap. "Call it a plan; they have more solidity; I love a plan."

The value of that plan is priceless. A road to walk down, a north star to head toward. A plan of action given wings by her gift of hope.

Your Network Tribe of One

"Associate only with positive, focused people who you can learn from and who will not drain your valuable energy with uninspiring attitudes. By developing relationships with those committed to constant improvement and the pursuit of the best that life has to offer, you will have plenty of company on your path to the top of whatever mountain you seek to climb."

– Author Robin Sharma

The amazing thing is we can have a tribe of inspiring people without ever meeting them in the flesh. Through LinkedIn, Twitter (that was), Facebook and audio books, you can find inspiring success stories, expand your library of knowledge, and nurture your creative thinking. Listen to audiobooks/podcasts/comedy shows when you are commuting and/or relaxing. Follow smart people and those who you can learn from on social media channels. This makes the world seem like one very small place. One big tribe that can influence, help, and power us on.

When I wanted to see how to get my first book published, I reached out to author EL James after reading how she self-published *50 Shades of Grey*. I wondered if that could be an option for me. She came straight back to me with a personal tweet about how she had had managed to get her book published with useful advice. It was really helpful and made me realise how much help was out there if you ask

The world is one amazingly connected place. Embrace it!

NOW TAKE ACTION!

Ask yourself the following to find your tribe:

1/ Why are we friends?
2/ What is it about you that I know you would be there for me no matter what?
3/ Look for those who have helped you in difficult times.
4/ Let go of those who have left you behind in difficult times.
5/ Avoid those who have been the cause of your difficult times.

FEARLESS WOMEN
Leanne Pero MBE

"Courage knows no boundaries; be bold, engage fearlessly, and defy conventions. Forge connections, for within each stranger lies the potential for transformative opportunities. Embrace fear, as it holds the key to unlocking unparalleled success."

— Leanne Pero MBE

I met Leanne through my work as an ambassador for the breast cancer charity Future Dreams and was instantly struck by her fearlessness. Leanne is an entrepreneur, model, former dancer, author, mentor and cancer survivor – and she is awesome. Her story underscores the remarkable strength of the human spirit and the transformative power of resilience.

After enduring a history of sexual abuse and leaving her family home at the age of 13, she discovered a love for dance and began inspiring young people to make a difference. When she was just 15, she launched a community-focused dance company, The Movement Factory, and found herself in a role of support and guidance. Those skills became cornerstones of her life's work and later inspired her to establish the cancer charity Black Women Rising.

Despite her achievements, Leanne's adult life hasnot been without its challenges. Her traumatic past initially led her to freeze on stage during performances, but through therapy and introspection, she discovered it was linked to post-traumatic stress disorder (PTSD). She candidly shared her battle with PTSD stemming from her traumatic childhood. Therapy became a vital tool, offering a secure space to address her trauma. Through an inner journey of learning and growing, Leanne reshaped her narrative and followed a path of healing and discovery. Leanne's ability to confront fear and seek healing exemplifies her strength.

"I derive immense satisfaction from witnessing people living their best lives. That's what I'm truly passionate about. I love that."

— Leanne Pero MBE

A pivotal moment in Leanne's life occurred with a cancer diagnosis.

Post-cancer, she struggled with the fear of it returning – only shifting her perspective after reading self-help book written by Louise Hay. She confronted her mortality, changed her perspective, and started to be less self-critical. She told me she embraced authenticity, pursued her dreams, and leveraged her gifts more, all of which combined to help her let go of fear and embrace a positive outlook.

Her own trauma also inspired the creation of a supportive community for others navigating similar challenges. What also stood out to her was the lack of physical and emotional support being provided by the NHS for black cancer patients. Leanne knew something had to change. She began arranging informal peer support groups for BAME female cancer patients and survivors: and so was born Black Women Rising, a transformative community empowering black women facing cancer. Through shared stories and experiences, she empowered women to tap into their inner strength and rewrite their narratives.

Leanne's story highlights the transformative potential of adversity. Her journey from trauma to empowerment is characterised by her unwavering spirit, dedication to aiding others, and her ability to harness gratitude and intention. Through her initiatives, Leanne is leaving a legacy. Her journey serves as a testament to the potential of channelling fear into positive action. Her story stands as an inspiring example of how embracing one's past and leveraging it as a catalyst for growth can lead to a future defined by resilience, purpose, and empowerment.

"My aspiration is to leverage my experiences to create greatness, not just for myself, but for my community and others."

— Leanne Pero MBE

My highlight this year was seeing *Unseen Unheard* at Theatre Peckham in London, which told the breast stories of Black women in the UK. The play was based on the lives of six women from Black Women Rising. It was honest, funny and produced real objectives around changing habits that will undoubtedly save future lives.

"My inner voice, God and the universe is why this has happened. I believe that each of us is on this earth to fulfil a purpose, and I firmly believe that my work here is aligned with that purpose. The trauma I've endured has driven me to create these transformational experiences and spaces, particularly through Black Women Rising."

— Leanne Pero MBE

Leanne's three tips for managing fear

1. **"Embrace intentional gratitude":** Leanne emphasises the practice of starting each day with a few deep breaths and a gratitude reflection. She finds 10 things to be grateful for and focuses on them. By acknowledging the positive aspects of life and focusing on what one already has, fear loses its grip and allows space for optimism and courage to emerge.
2. **"Stay present and centered":** Leanne suggests a simple yet profound technique for managing fear in the moment and bringing oneself into the present. Just remind yourself, she says, that "right now, everything is okay. "This practice centers the mind and prevents anxiety from becoming overwhelming.
3. **"Breathe and reset":** Through conscious and intentional breathing, fear dissipates, making way for

clarity and a more balanced perspective. This practice, combined with resetting one's thoughts, offers a chance to regain control over emotions.

STEP 6: (EN)LIGHTEN

"Out of your vulnerabilities will come your strength."

– Sigmund Freud

The sixth step is about feeling and living a more enlightened life or living a lighter life. Most people think of the Buddha when they hear that mysterious word "enlightened." But in practice, "lighten" means practicing a few simple things that make your life feel lighter. I mean lighter in your mind, body, and soul. Then you need to make these things a habit and a pattern you can maintain daily.

These things will give you a new strategy to navigate obstacles, and this will make you more creative, curious, and lighter. You will be able to take on new opportunities for growth. When you have a lighter way of living and moving forward, you find more harmony and are less burdened by fear or the past. You will be looking at the world in a new way, and the world needs a fresh new approach because what we have been doing to date is not working for us or our planet.

Reflect now on the plans, goals, visions, and values that we spoke about in earlier exercises. This will help you step into a lighter zone, where real growth happens, and you can start living an extraordinary life. But a warning here – don't get stuck in the planning stage. Use the foundation as a launchpad. You need to take action! I promise you, in one year, you will not believe the difference.

We are in an era of pioneers. No one really knows what will come next, how the world will change, and what it will look like tomorrow. But one thing we know is we can't go back. Bold, brave ideas need to come to life. If you are in a boring job and you hate it, think about what freedom you could have if you feel lighter.

I mentioned earlier that I started running my first business aged 31, with a nine-month-old baby in tow. My friend and I decided to go it alone. It was scary on so many levels. But I was ready for change and wanted the freedom that being a business owner could give me. I'll never forget walking into the bank, and the bank advisor asking us how much we thought we would make in that first year. We had no idea it would be a six-figure sum! But we dared to dream, and crazy things happened when we got behind that belief.

But first and ultimately, you need to do some of the heavy lifting so that you can feel lighter. These few things I've found to be helpful to my coaching clients and myself can transform your perspective and the weight of responsibility you try to carry on a daily basis

Don’t try Daily to EAT an Elephant (live in the present moment)

Attempting to devour an elephant-sized load of tasks on a daily basis is like trying to bite off more than you can chew – quite literally! Now, don't get me wrong, I'm not asking you to take this literally. Rather, I'm a fan of metaphors, and they paint a strong visual image, particularly when I'm coaching. When I tell them to "Stop trying to eat an elephant," it's like a sudden jolt that catches them off guard.

You see, people often stuff an overwhelming amount of tasks into their days, only to find themselves drowning in stress, feeling disheartened, and even becoming a tad harsh on themselves. It's a vicious cycle that goes completely against the notion of lightness.

Take this one instance when I was working with this incredible supermom – two energetic kids, a full-time job, and she was even diving into her own business venture on the side. One day, she reached out to me in a state of frenzy, desperately seeking guidance. "I'm swamped," she confessed during our call, her voice trembling. "I need to rev up my PR, give my social media a kick, whip up a new design for my product, craft catchy copy for my website, snag 3 or 4 articles in the press to launch my product, gather a solid fan base through website sign-ups, knock on retailers' doors to showcase my product, AND sort out those sample orders!"

"Whoa, slow down," I exclaimed... It felt like OTT – Overwhelming, Traumatic, and Threatening to her well-being.

She was practically suffocating under the weight of her own expectations, convinced she was failing miserably. Oh, and she casually added that her daughter was sick, she'd been up all night, and her husband was away on business. My jaw nearly dropped at the mountain of responsibility she was carrying.

That's when I dished out my "Stop trying to eat an elephant" line. The line hung in the air for a moment, and then she burst into laughter. It was as if I'd shaken her out of a heavy trance. "You're basically tackling a colossal elephant of tasks all at once," I explained. "Let's rethink this." I urged her to unload the burden, make a list, and break those Herculean tasks into bite-sized pieces. I advised her to highlight the key priorities, and then I nudged her to allot a little time each day for this mammoth endeavour. "What's your schedule like?" I inquired. "Can you carve out 1.5 hours daily for this, or perhaps enlist some backup to lighten the load?"

Now, don't misunderstand me. Keeping your eyes on the prize – your grand vision, your purpose, your mission – is crucial as you mould the life you desire. But here's the kicker: you've got to do it with a dollop of self-kindness in the present moment. The key is to slice that grand vision into manageable morsels, ensuring you're not grappling with an elephant-sized mess. Avoid the overwhelm, the sinking feeling of being burdened, and the discontent that comes with it. Initially, you'll feel as fragile as a snowflake, but as this practice becomes second nature, your personal boundaries will stand tall, and you'll find that buoyant sense of lightness.

Personally, I uncover life's lightness by embracing the here and now with a dash of playfulness. Trust me, I've wasted months fretting over mortality and fearing my business might tank. It's like squandering precious moments of existence. So, I've invested years – delved into my life's lessons, earned coaching credentials, and soaked up various other courses – all in the pursuit of mastering these strategies. It's an ongoing journey, a daily expedition to unearth your inner power and nourish your inner wisdom. Think of it like a cup that perpetually needs refilling. If you're aiming to become tougher, more resilient, and audaciously fearless, do this...

FEARLESS THINKING... So you don't eat an elephant when you're overwhelmed.

1: **List it out:** Compile a comprehensive to-do list to clear the mental clutter.

2: **Priorities:** Separate tasks into urgent and non-urgent, setting realistic deadlines.

3: Schedule time: Allocate specific daily slots for task completion

4: **Break it down:** Divide tasks into smaller, manageable steps for easy progress.

Embracing these steps, you'll find that lightening the load is about strategically conquering challenges rather than doing everything at once.

Meditation: You Can Choose Your Thought

"We conducted a study with novice mediators and were curious to observe what biological changes would occur in just one week of intensive practice. We analysed 2882 metabolites, and after 7 days, almost 100% of the novice mediators showed significant biological changes in their blood. These changes suggested they were experiencing a different internal environment. Interestingly, they were situated in a ballroom, but the changes were occurring within them. The source of these chemicals was their own internal systems. Their intentions and emotional states triggered the production of various chemicals. The connection between how we think, and feel can profoundly alter things in our lives."

- *Joe Dispenza*

I'm not sure at what point I realised my heavy thoughts were ruining my life. It could have been the worry of setting up a business, getting breast cancer, having a premature baby, being in a male-dominated industry, and feeling as a woman I wasn't good enough, thinking my words and thoughts had no value. It was a culmination of many things. But one day, I decided to change my thought pattern and shine! To do this, I decided to study mindfulness and meditation.

I took the time out of life to visit a dear friend at an ashram in India. I learned how to meditate and how meditation frees your mind from the noise of unruly thoughts. Before this point, I felt that there was a 'dark art' to meditation that I would never grasp. They taught us a few different types: meditation of sound, touch, and sight.

Practice 1 - Sound: Close your eyes and hear a noise far, far away and focus on this noise. I tend to listen to birdsong, focusing all of my attention on the cheeps and chirps for 60 seconds. Then focus on a noise close to you, like your own breathing, do this for 60 seconds or more.

Practice 2 – Touch: I walk into the garden and simply focus all my attention on a leaf for one minute. I look at its colour, the river of veins in its texture, and run my fingers over its tiny hairs.

Practice 3 – Sight: I lie under a tree in my garden for 15 minutes studying its trunk and running my eyes up one of the thick branches, along the tiny branches, and into the buds of life at the end. Every time my chattering mind tries to talk, I focus on the trunk of the tree and start the journey again. At times I chant my positive affirmations.

This whole session can last for a few minutes, but it's so grounding. When I was going through my panic with the cancer diagnosis, I found that going into the garden and touching a leaf, or lying under a tree and watching the trunk all the way up to the tips of the branches lightened my mind. This is a form of "Tree bathing" which has become super popular in parks across the UK.

Meditation offers a wide range of benefits that contribute to overall well-being and mental clarity. These include: **Stress Reduction:** Engaging in meditation helps activate the body's relaxation response, alleviating stress and promoting a sense of calm. **Improved Focus:** Regular practice enhances concentration and attention, leading to better productivity and cognitive function. **Emotional Balance:** Meditation can reduce symptoms of anxiety and depression, fostering emotional resilience and a greater sense of happiness. **Self-Awareness:** By observing thoughts and feelings without judgment, meditation encourages self-reflection and a deeper understanding of oneself. **Mind-Body Connection:** Meditation strengthens the link between mental and physical well-being, promoting better self-care. **Blood Pressure Regulation:** Through relaxation and stress reduction, meditation helps maintain healthy blood pressure levels. **Quality Sleep:** Meditation's calming effects contribute to improved sleep quality and insomnia management. **Pain Management:** Mindfulness meditation can alter pain perception and tolerance, offering relief for chronic pain conditions. **Compassion Cultivation:** Some practices focus on kindness and compassion, fostering better relationships and a more positive outlook. **Brain Health:** Studies suggest meditation positively influences brain structure, connectivity, and cognitive function.

Regular meditation yields these benefits, supporting a healthier and more balanced lifestyle.

FEARLESS THINKING. Meditation

1: Try meditating with touch.

2: Try meditation with sight

3; Try meditation with sounds

One of my favourite meditation apps is "MEDITATIONS for Breaking the Habit" by Dr. Joe Dispenza. His book "Becoming Supernatural" is profound and well worth a read.

Rethink your limiting beliefs

Challenging and stopping your own limiting beliefs can make you feel lighter and more empowered. Limiting beliefs are negative thought patterns or perceptions that hold you back from reaching your full potential or hinder your progress. These beliefs can create a sense of heaviness, self-doubt, and emotional burden. When you actively work to identify and change these limiting beliefs, you free yourself from the mental constraints that have been weighing you down. I had three limiting beliefs that have at times become big obstacles that I've worked daily to overcome.

Belief 1: The first is that my business ventures would fail.

Belief 2: That we as a family would run out of money.

Belief 3: Life was futile. What was the point, after 2 aggressive cancers, was it worth it?

My first belief is because being the daughter of a social worker and a teacher, how could I ever be a successful entrepreneur or writer, I would ask myself.

The second was, as a family, we never had much money. I also worried I would run out of money. The third was, after the cancers, what was the point?

The consequence of having these limited beliefs was catastrophic. They stopped me trying, they kept me small, they became excuses, they stopped me from following my dreams, and the cancer belief was the worse as it stopped me from moving forward and just left me wallowing in the mud of fear. So, I flipped them one day because those limiting beliefs into truths and affirmations.

Belief 1: My business ventures would fail. NO

New belief, Affirmation 1: I will succeed in my new ventures and follow my passion! It worked!

Belief 2: We as a family would run out of money. NO

New belief, Affirmation 2: If I serve a higher good, energy = money will come in abundance. If I used my gifts and did my best, clients would pay me to help them. And they Did!

Belief 3: Life was futile.

New belief, Affirmation 3: Life is a gift. Shine as brightly as I can and hope my spirit and energy light up my friends, the people I meet, and my community. And I do!

If you decide today to flip your limited beliefs, it can change your life – it will make you feel lighter, more determined, and a light in yours, your family, and other people's lives. It will also lead to: **Increased confidence** – boosting your self-confidence as you realise that you can achieve more than you thought. It reduces stress and anxiety. **Reduced Stress and Anxiety:** Letting go of limiting beliefs can alleviate stress and anxiety because you're no longer dwelling on negative thoughts that contribute to these emotions. This can lead to a lighter and more relaxed mental state. **Improved Mental Well-being:** Replacing limiting beliefs with more positive and empowering ones contributes to overall mental well-being. You'll likely experience a greater sense of happiness, positivity, and emotional balance. **Increased Motivation and Productivity:** Letting go of limiting beliefs can ignite your motivation and productivity. When you believe in your abilities and potential, you're more likely to act and pursue your goals with determination. **Enhanced Relationships:** Limiting beliefs can also affect your interactions with others. By shedding these beliefs, you may find it easier to connect with people and build healthier relationships. **Openness to Opportunities:** As you challenge and change your limiting beliefs, you become more open to new opportunities and experiences that you might have previously dismissed or avoided.

FEARLESS THINKING. What are your limiting beliefs list them below:

Your limited Belief 1:

Your limited Belief 2:

Your limited Belief 3:

What's the consequence of these limited belief, how are they holding you back?

Now the fun part. Flip the limiting beliefs on their head, turn the new beliefs into daily affirmations and say them to yourself daily to make yourself feel lighter and more empowered.

New belief - Affirmation 1:

New belief - Affirmation 2:

New belief - Affirmation 3:

Dear Julia (a letter to myself)

Did I believe in myself 100% when I started my business? No! I was petrified. The risk of resigning from my old job with a new baby was huge, as was the worry of how much time I would have to give to that my new role while bringing up a child. Fast forward almost 20 years, if I could write a letter to my younger self, I would tell her the following:

1/ Spend time knowing what you want to stand for.

2/ Be kind to yourself

3/ Trust yourself. if you do your best and shine the money will come

4/ Don't work all hours, take time out to breathe and have ideas

5/ Build relationships with your tribe, focus on helping people, serving them as best as you can.

6/ Don't be scared to admit it when you mess up – none of us is perfect.

7/ Use technology – it will save wasted time Keep your head in building relationships, building communities offering help This is the best way technology can help you. Build the community and you will always have work, referrals and people that want to work with you.

8/ Make time for yourself and walk, run, do yoga it will relax you.

9/ Make time for your family, switch off the phone, be there for your kids.

10/ Follow your passions, stay curious and creative.

11/ Surround yourself with the right people, they will light you up!.

12/ Stopping thinking so much and make it happen. Do it NOW!

13/ You don't know what you don't know, so ask for help along the way.

14/ Mentor and be mentored, learn from the best and give back when you can.

15/ Don't be scared of change, it will happen when you least expect it.

16/ Create boundaries and don't be afraid of saying no.

17/ Most of all, enjoy life and treat yourself along the way to an icecream.

FEARLESS THINKING...

Write a letter to your younger self: This exercise can be useful try it for yourself. It's so powerful to look back on in 2/3/5 years' time. It can unblock your negative patterns, take away the heaviness and make you feel lighter as a person;

Why bother?

Why did I take my healing journey and plan seriously? Because I wanted to live a new empowered life. A life clear of burdens, without fear and anxiety. To free myself to feel lighter and more colourful and creative. This took curiosity, a little courage, and bold planning. To lighten your load, you need to think deeply about how the next year can be different from the last year. If you want to feel lighter—what can you change?

With all your experience, gifts, values, and ideas, and your north star in mind, what will the next 1/3/5 years look like for you? Imagine this shining future fully. Take time to imagine the details of your vision and watch them take shape in your mind's eye. Then step into and live in your imagination for a while, where the real growth happens, and start to really feel what it means to be living an extraordinary life.

All of us have a need for boundaries to protect a healing body or mind, and this is also true when developing a healthy mindset...you need time for change to bed in and grow, to align, for you to have time to create the life you want with all your new and exciting plans.

Good mental and physical health is wealth, lightness, and love. Keep your vision, purpose, and mission for the future at the front of your mind when you are developing the lifestyle you want to have. You will feel delicate at first, but as it becomes habitual, your boundaries are protected, you will feel the lightness

FEARLESS THINKING…WHY, WHY NOT?

THERE ARE NO INCORRECT ANSWERS TO THESE QUESTIONS. THEY TELL YOU MORE ABOUT YOU:

1: WHY should I try in life? Why work hard, make friends, earn that much?

2: WHY NOT try?

what else are you going to do with your life?

Why not see what you can become?

3: Why me? Why NOT YOU?

Some people do so well, they see it all. If someone else gets to see London, be an author or have an acting career, then so can you.

4: When is right, Why NOT NOW?

Because now is a time to act as one with purpose, passion and future values. Create and stick to your big plan, set a new goal, lock onto a new resolve, do it now and work for yourself and the greater good.

NOW TAKE ACTION!

Embrace these guiding principles to lighten your load:

1. **Prioritise Tasks:** Break down tasks, prioritise them as urgent or non-urgent, and allocate specific time slots for completion.
2. **Meditate:** Start a daily meditation practice using techniques like sound, touch, and sight meditation.
3. **Challenge Limiting Beliefs:** Identify and flip three limiting beliefs into positive affirmations. Repeat affirmations daily.
4. **Create Boundaries:** Set clear boundaries to protect your well-being and create space for growth.
5. **Visualise Your Ideal Life:** Spend time daily visualising your ideal, enlightened life.
6. **Practice Self-Compassion:** Treat yourself with kindness and self-love. Let go of self-criticism.
7. **Share Your Journey:** Engage in meaningful conversations with others to share experiences and insights.
8. **Embrace Curiosity and Creativity:** Cultivate a mindset of curiosity, learning, and exploration.
9. **Take Small Positive Actions:** Choose one small action daily to make a positive impact on your life or others'.
10. **Reflect on Your Progress:** Regularly reflect on your journey and the positive changes you've experienced.

Remember, these key action points can help you create a lighter and more enlightened life. Start with a few that resonate with you, and gradually incorporate more as you feel comfortable. Implement these steps and watch your life transform with newfound empowerment and purpose.

STEP 7: ONENESS

"People who believe in oneness -- the idea that everything in the world is connected and interdependent -- appear to have greater life satisfaction than those who don't, regardless of whether they belong to a religion or don't."

—The American Psychological Association.

https://www.sciencedaily.com/releases/2019/04/

The idea of oneness alone is mind-blowing. Sometimes we can get a sense or feeling of oneness that makes the tiny hairs on our neck and hands stand on end. This is often accompanied by a feeling of **flow** *and* **correctness**—the sense that everything is working as it should. We are most likely to experience this feeling when we are doing something extraordinary. Top athletes, musicians, writers, dancers, surgeons, artists and astronauts, all report experiencing this amazing sensation when they are doing something they love and have practiced until it felt perfectly natural and easy.

Oneness is an incredibly comforting and awe-inspiring idea. Everything in the universe is part of a continually turning and churning machine that recycles everything over and over but never repeats. What is more, everything is linked in a chain of cause and effect so great that each part, big or small, is in some way connected to every other. So, the idea of **oneness** is really the other side of the coin with the concept of **endlessness** or **infinity**—so, we are all connected, but not just in the local, here and now—we are also connected over vast, unimaginably huge, potentially-endless stretches of space and time.

It is common for meditators, yoga or martial artists to experience the same sense of oneness when in the flow of their practice, and here the feeling of connection with the energy of the planet is very strong. Gardening can be an incredibly beneficial activity for many healthy reasons, including the way you physically interact with plants and the earth, cementing that feeling of oneness with a rich, multi-sensory experience of immersion with Nature. Finally, people in the throes of religious ecstasy have reported that the feelings of oneness, connection, flow and awe all come together when sensing the overwhelming and powerful presence of the Divine. All of us are humbled and uplifted at the same time when we see a new-born baby—and giving birth to new life is the best example of oneness anyone could ever experience.

You Are a Star!

"It's a great human-interest story that we are now able to map the abundance of all of the major elements found in the human body across hundreds of thousands of stars in our Milky Way."

—Prof. Jennifer Johnson, Science Team Chair SDSS-III APOGEE survey

Oneness is a common thread that we all share with each other, like the fact that we are made up of the same atomic building blocks as stars. The elements that make up our bodies, such as carbon, nitrogen, hydrogen and oxygen were created through nuclear fusion in the cores of stars, billions of years ago. When those stars finally exploded as supernovas, they scattered the elements into space where they eventually coalesced into new planets and life forms. That is why we can say truly we are all made of stardust!

Connected: A complex but beautiful tapestry of our life

We are all creatures of the Earth, intrinsically and emotionally connected together (I wrote a fiction book called "Colourful Creatures" which I will be re-releasing this year, expanding on this concept).These connections are invisible bonds that weave together to create a vast tapestry of life. Whether we know it or not, each one of us is a gift to those around us, helping each other be who we are and weaving a collective picture. Imagine these connections coming to life, appearing as hundreds of bright, red pulsating ribbons binding us together, wrapping around our bodies, minds, and souls. Our happiness and the boundless loving energy from our positive connections make the ribbons illuminate the night sky with sparkling, electrical currents running back and forth between them. There is no "I" in this world, only "we." This is the world I yearn for, the world of unity.

Each day, we forge new connections and attach new ribbons, gradually weaving a dynamic picture that pulsates and changes with the seasons of our lives. This is our world.

Humans are not separate entities from what we call "nature." We are very much a part of nature – inside it, intricately woven into it. Modern life has often caused our kinship and interconnection with the natural world to be forgotten, ignored, and suppressed. However, remembering who and what we are can bring about a radical, magical shift in our perspective and self-understanding. It can help us feel more grounded, purposeful, significant, and beautiful. Connecting with nature can evoke a sense of oneness with everything in the universe, allowing us to recognise ourselves as profoundly spiritual beings. This connection brings peace, contentment, and a deep sense of knowing – something everyone desires. You can foster this connection by meditating in a natural setting, planting trees or flowers, gardening, growing your own food, hiking, or engaging in wild swimming.

Look After Your Garden

Have you noticed that when you go out and mow the lawn, do some weeding and planting, your neighbours come out one by one and start doing the same! Soon your whole street is lined with beautifully tended gardens! If we look after our own health, and the health of our tribes, businesses and gardens, we will all become wealthier in mind, body and soul, becoming more empowered. When we make the inward change, it ripples out-wards, creating harmony in the world. A new era. Radiate the new you into your community, the people around you, your work colleagues, the people in the street. When your love and joy start to flow outwards, you will feel it radiate back to you. You will see a profound effect on your own inner light and on others.

When we are at one, we don't feel lonely or disconnected, we feel part of the whole, part of a tribe and part of the universal bigger picture. We can tap into this feeling of oneness with our sixth sense, the creative vision of our subconscious mind, through which ideas, plans, and thoughts flash into our consciousness. Those 'hunches' or 'inspirations' you sometimes ignore are usually coded messages from your subconscious to look a bit closer. Like all living beings, we have infinite intelligence inside our DNA – the instructions that combined our atoms into our bodies and grows acorns into trees, and for 4 billion years evolved our planet into a living, breathing, connected world.

On a micro level, we are comprised of billions of human cells and ten times as many friendly micro-organisms that keep our gut and our skin healthy. There as many micro-organisms in your body or in the soil of your garden as bright stars in the Milky Way Galaxy. Without those micro-organisms, our gardens and our bodies would not function correctly. We are inter-connected, we are symbiotic. The parts and the whole are one. Every living thing is a delicately balanced eco-system of millions of smaller organisms coexisting and relying on each other for survival. There are many fantastic sci-fi books and films that show how the macroscopic and microscopic worlds all play out as their own complete eco-system. As above, so below. On a macro level, how we act as part of the eco-system of this planet is directly connected to the agriculture and ecology of other parts of the world and affects every other species.

Nature is full of energy and so are you. If we start to think as ONE within ourselves e.g., in our mind, body, and soul, our parts become more unified and connected. We start to become more aware of our bodies. We can learn to meditate, scan, and listen to our bodies to understand what they need. When I took a Reiki Course, this was taught as a 'power practice'.

When you are going through a cancer diagnosis and treatment, most of the battle is **feeling** at ONE with your mind, body and soul and **believing** that each one of your cells will be well. Wish them loving energy every day, learn to read the signals, our own body's language.

FEARLESS THINKING... Look after your garden exercise

I love this workshop that I do with clients.

STEP 1:

Close your eyes and visualise yourself a garden with 5 different sections.

Each section represents a different part of your emotional, creative, mental, physical, spiritual self. Your job is to water it and give It special nutrients and the care it needs to make it grow. As each part blooms and grows to its fullest its more in harmony with the other sections and this increases the beauty of the whole eco-system.

Example: This shows the 5 areas of the garden.

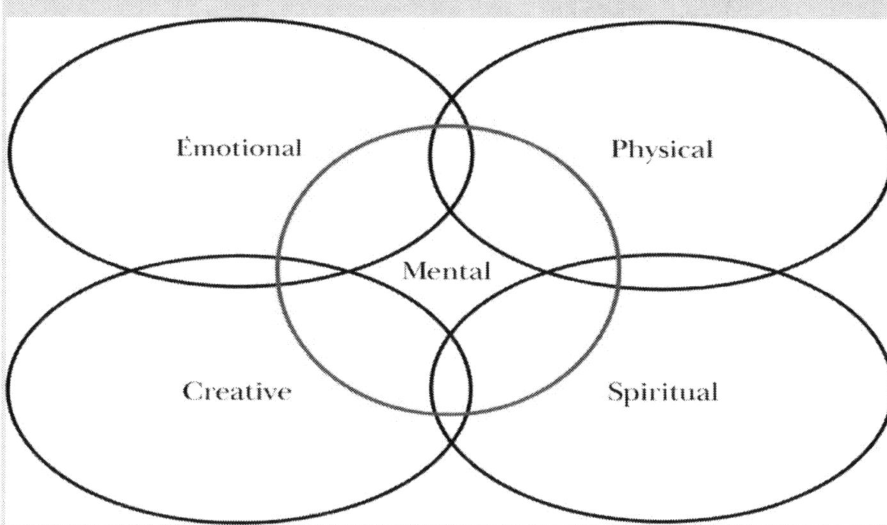

Ask yourself?

Which part of the garden has been most neglected by you and needs more care, love, water and attention. Why and what made it less important?

STEP 2:

Think of a programme to upgrade this one section of the garden. There is no right or wrong way, only the best for you a unique colourful, wonderful one of a kind human being.

Write a programme for this one section there is no right diet, exercise, medication, love, joy or creation only the best for you!

Example:

In this example the "Creative" section of the garden is barren.

Creativity is the ability to use imagination, originality, and innovative thinking to generate new ideas, concepts, or solutions to problems. Creativity increases positive emotions + reduces anxiety. Thinking creatively opens up your heart and mind. This helps improve the function of your immune system and making your trillion cells ☺

If the creative part of your garden needs nurturing how would you nurture your creative nature? e.g go to art galleries, experiment and take risks? take a drawing class, learn to do pottery or learnt to dance? Collaborate with others? Embrace imperfection?

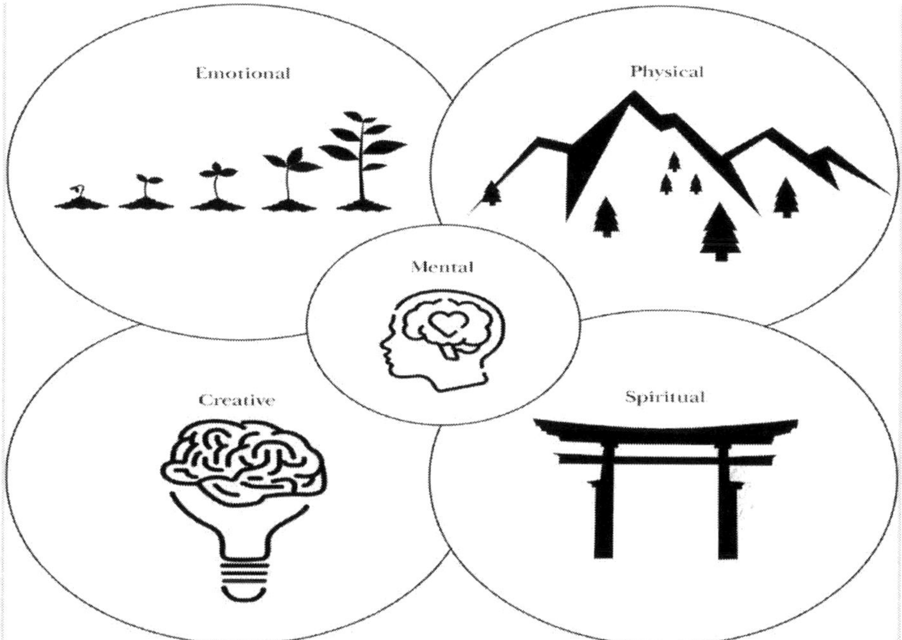

Other areas to discover….

Emotional health : Understand your feelings, express healthily, bond positively, self-care, seek therapy.

Physical health : Exercise, healthy diet, more sleep, reduce anxiety, limit alcohol.

Mental health : Practice Self-care, Seek social support, engage in enjoyable activities, seek therapy, practice mindfulness, set realistic goals

Spiritually health: Practice gratitude, reflect on beliefs and values, connect with nature, seek out like minded communities, engage in acts of service.

For further reading Joe Dispenza's book "Becoming Supernatural" is excellent and worth a read.

Staying in Oneness (love expands, fear shrinks)

When doing any physical activity, keeping part of our awareness on our bodies helps us to perform better. Similarly, when meditating or practicing movements, staying in the body and feelings allows old, stagnant patterns to bubble up to the surface of our awareness. Mental and physical knots unclench and unwind through natural movement if we relax into them and express ourselves. Sometimes we need the help of a professional therapist or coach to work out these weaknesses safely and fully. The very best performers and athletes (like Anna) inspire us because they show us our own potential as fellow humans. But what we don't always hear about is what it took to work out all their own stumbling blocks through coaching and practice and injuries and healing.

If you are already familiar with being in the flow state, when you are performing or rehearsing something and it just goes perfectly, you will probably also know how easily sudden distractions or obstacles can snap us out of the flow state and literally trip us up!

Similarly, negative thoughts or unresolved memories can instantly pull us out of our immersion in oneness.

So, when the Fear Monster pops up again suddenly, it makes us halt and move backwards, shrink back and not move forward. We have to face it, listen to it, feel the exchange and movement of energy, and move on. Now, it is the fear monster that shrinks back down again, or evaporates like vapour, or transforms like a frog into a prince! Yes, it's like magic!

Something surprising, out of place or disruptive can instantly distract us from our flow and our purpose. It can pull us straight out of oneness and flow into separate-ness and awkwardness. Suddenly, we hesitate and are unsure of ourselves, we brace ourselves for an accident or problem and tighten up. Negativity is so destructive, as you know, it wastes time, exhausts us and makes us sabotage healthy relationships. It's also a story we tell ourselves that isn't proven, e.g., fear lives in the past or future, not in what is actually real in the here and now. This is especially true in working environments and business relationships, where it is taboo to talk about your feelings.

When we act more as one in our organisations at work, our local community, our country, our planet we are all pushing in the same direction, respecting the same values, and achieving the same goals together. We function as one. Each arm of the organisation is like the arm of an octopus (an octopus has three brains to control its arms and skin camouflage as well as the main one in its head.

Businesses spends millions on creating a vision, a mantra, values and an approach to unite its workforce behind one powerful vision—*'Just do it'* as Nike says. It gives **internal** direction and empowers its employees and, at the same time, creates a very positive **external** image that customers find attractive and want to wear on their bodies. The values and the image of the business and its products are all in alignment. This then influences the buyers of the product who share the brand values. In this way, the message in the brand ripples out and populates the world. This is true of any sphere of commerce or exchange.

We are all interconnected on this one beautiful earth—our one home.

When we understand the power of acting as ONE, we can all work together harmoniously to create a healthy future for everyone. We can save this planet and develop it so we all have a future. Remember that the life force within you and your millions of atoms, protons, molecules is the same universal energy and force that flows throughout the universe. The atoms that exist in your body were once created in the furnace of a star.

Kabir, an Indian saint and poet of the 15th century, described oneness as both the **one** (the water) and the **many** (the waves) being the **same** (the river).

"The river and the waves are one surf: where is the difference between the river and the waves? When the wave rises, it is the water; and when it falls, it is the same water again. Tell me, Sir, where is the distinction? Because it has been named as wave, shall it no longer be considered as water?"

—Kabir, 15th Century Indian poet & saint

Reflection:

To understand and consider how you are part of the harmony and flow of the universe, how you are part of one ecosystem and what that means to you. So that I treat you in the same way I treat myself with the same love and respect, because I am part of the same universe.

The Story of my Guardian Angel and the power of Invisible Counsellors

In the famous book "Think and Grow Rich," by Napoleon Hill which sold 100m copies world-wide it mentions the concept of "Invisible Counsellors." These counsellors are a technique Hill suggests for tapping into the collective wisdom and knowledge of great thinkers, historical figures, and individuals you admire. The idea is to create a mental council of these personalities and engage in imaginary conversations with them to seek guidance, inspiration, and insights. This concept is presented as a method for developing ideas, solving problems, and gaining new perspectives to achieve success and personal growth.

I have created using his concept my own Invisible Counsellors and built my own imaginary team – Louise Hay and Jacqueline Gold are two of many. When I'm on a walk in the forest near my house I ask for their wisdom and wonder what they would say to help me with my challenges.

Do you believe in a universe that's guiding you, or a guardian angel who's on your side? Over the years it's given me great comfort to think that I'm being watched over – either by a loved one who has passed away or simply the energy in the universe. There are times in life when I have been at my lowest and someone has unexpectedly spoken to me with such a wisdom that it has triggered my sixth sense and feeling of oneness.

In the days leading up to my five-year cancer checks, I hid my pain and sadness, even from myself. I repressed my anger, denied my vulnerability, took care of everyone else's needs and denied myself my own. Only five years after being diagnosed with cancer I'd fallen back into old ways and put myself to the bottom of the pile. I wasn't in the flow, and I'd not been filling my cup.

Me time was a tiny sliver carved out of a huge rock. I had made the mistake of going to the hospital appointment alone, and that loneliness had meant I cried on my own and panicked on my own. When I left the hospital with my bad news – that the cancer had come back again – I walked to the underground in a trance. I was surrounded by people but I was still all alone and my sadness saturated the carriage of the train. Unaware of the tube slowing, I didn't notice a woman jump on board just as the doors were closing. Then I realised that the woman was trying to catch my eye.

"I used to be sad too," she said, her voice thick with a Polish accent.

I looked around to see who she was talking to. Everyone in the carriage looked into their phones, ignoring us. *Bloody candy Crush.* I could never work out why it was being played on every sodding screen I could see. Such a stupid use of time, life and energy. *"Time is all we have so make good use of it,"* the woman whispered, as if reading my mind. She then reached over and tapped my hand with one of her fingernails.

'I used to work 12- or 13-hour days, and I was sad too. I never thought of me," she said. "Now I only work four hours a day as a cleaner."

For a few seconds her fingers settled on my shaking hand. Just as I was about to pull away, she added, "You will be alright my love. You are being looked after." I suddenly felt a calm sensation flush through my body.

"Alright"' I thought. "Would I be alright?" The words felt good in my mind. "Alright. Alright. Alright."

Up until then I wasn't sure if I believed in guardian angels, but I had an overwhelming feeling that I was open and in-tune with the universe and it had heard my cry and helped. It was so random; I had never met her before and she was giving me comfort and a new energy that tingled in my hand and through my body. She had spoken about the exact topic I had in my head. As I turned to respond she jumped off the tube and waved.

"Alright. Alright. Alright. I'm going to be alright!" I tuned out my anxiety with this positive mantra, seeking relief in this lifelong habit with the knowledge that the universe and my guardian angel was looking after me. contentment, and knowingness – who wouldn't want that?

FEARLESS THINKING... Guardian Angel

Have you ever felt that you have a guardian angel helping you or any invisible counselors that can help you? It's a powerful exercise to engage in creative visualisation and mental dialogue with your chosen figures to draw upon their collective wisdom and guidance.

Walking In our own Inner Nature (but then feeling as one)

Each of us is born into a universe entirely our own, where a myriad of emotions and experience- fear, growth, joy, sadness, hope, pride, regret, love, and even hatred- reside. This unique universe, often portrayed by spiritual leaders and writers as an essential component of the human ecosystem, frequently conceals certain aspects of our lives, even from our closest friends. At times, these distinctive worlds are shrouded in secrecy, while at others, they are openly exhibited to the wolrd.

The moments when I truly embrace a profound sense of unity and oneness are those spent immersed in nature, engaging in yoga, practicing meditation, and partaking in activities that allow me to sync with the universe's rhythm. These are instances when I feel most connected and attuned to the flow of existence. In such states of oneness, loneliness and detachment dissolve, replaced by a profound belongingness to the entirety of creation. It's as though I'm an integral part of a vast cosmic tribe, woven into the grand tapestry of the universe.

Embracing our collective power to function as a unified entity opens the door to shaping a brighter tomorrow. Recognising that the life force coursing through us – comprised of countless atoms, protons, and particles – is intrinsically intertwined with the very energy that courses through the cosmos, empowers us. Armed with this awareness, we can bravely dive into the cosmic ocean, relishing its flow, dynamism, and thrill. Seizing hold of this cosmic force propels us to soar to new heights. Trust me, I've ventured there myself.

FEARLESS THINKING...

Try taking a walk in nature and thinking about your own inner universe and how it's connected with the home we live on.

The Starfish Story

Over the last two years, I've been writing a novel called "Mother of all Gods, Men, and Earth." It's one of my biggest undertakings yet, as it's about the story of Mother Nature as a real woman living amongst us (imagine that!). It's involved a lot of deep research into the planet, our future on the planet, and how we are all interconnected. It's been overwhelming but also enlightening and mind-blowing.

Science and religion are converging as we begin to recognise our oneness. A book called the "Tao of Physics" by Fritjof Capra talks about the connection between quantum physics (developments in the last 60 years) and ancient eastern mysticism, emphasising our interconnection. Newton's view of us as a solid universe has shifted, and we now know everything is, in fact, made of atoms. Each atom contains space, movement, and energy, revealing our interconnectedness, and like the stars, we are made up of the same ingredients. Eastern mystics from thousands of years ago had already grasped this dynamic understanding.

"The Gaia Hypothesis" proposed by James Lovelock in 1972 views Earth as a single organism, with every living thing working together for survival. Our separation harms it; we must align with this universal flow. Earth isn't solely a protector but a fragile system. We're pushing its limits. Our purpose must support sustainability and biodiversity, benefiting all. Recognising our shared humanity fosters empathy, transcending differences. Unity, love, and joy become central. In this interconnected world, harmonious coexistence is paramount.

These books have profoundly shaped my life and my understanding of the oneness of all things, and they might help you recognise why we get those senses or feelings of oneness that make the tiny hairs on our neck and hands stand on end. This is often accompanied by a feeling of flow and correctness—the sense that everything is working as it should. One day last year, I read the enduring tale of "The Starfish Story," a narrative that retains its profound impact no matter how often I read it. It makes me feel part of a oneness in the world and really think about the part I can play in society without getting and feeling overwhelmed.

In a time long ago, there dwelt an elderly gentleman who sought solace and inspiration by the tranquil shores of the ocean. With the dawn of each new day, before delving into his creative pursuits, he embarked on a leisurely stroll along the sun-kissed beach. On a particular morning, following the departure of a tumultuous storm, he ventured out to find the coastline adorned with a mesmerising sight – a vast expanse of starfish, adorning the sands as far as the eye could behold.

In the distance, a young boy captured his attention, his actions punctuating the serene landscape. As the boy drew closer, the observer noted his intermittent pauses and the graceful motions of bending down. With each step, it became apparent that he was lifting these celestial creatures and casting them into the embrace of the sea. Intrigued by this benevolent endeavour, the man extended his greeting, "Good morning! Might I inquire about the noble pursuit that engages you?"

The youthful boy paused, his gaze meeting the man's, and he responded with unwavering sincerity, "I'm granting freedom to these starfish, returning them to the ocean's realm. Stranded by the tide upon the shore, they lack the means to navigate the journey back to their watery sanctuary. When the sun ascends its throne in the sky, their fate is sealed unless I intervene, offering them passage to the waves." A brief contemplative moment passed before the elderly man raised a sceptical inquiry, "Yet this beach is strewn with countless starfish, a multitude that seems insurmountable. Can your efforts truly yield a meaningful impact?"

Unfazed by doubt, the boy gracefully bent down, his hand enveloping another starfish, and with an intentional toss, he propelled it into the expansive ocean. Turning back to meet the man's gaze, a radiant smile spread across his face as he proclaimed, "To that singular starfish, my action has made an indelible difference!"

This timeless tale, inspired by Loren Eisele's "The Star Thrower," resonates deeply with each of us. It serves as a poignant reminder of our capacity to ignite positive change that can literally change the world and make each one of us feel lighter.

There come moments, much akin to my own experiences, where doubt creeps in, the load feels heavy – a whisper questioning the impact of my endeavours amidst bustling lives. Such moments intensify when we confront daunting global challenges like hunger or the quest for a cure for afflictions like cancer. Why can't we act more and be more one? Yet, this narrative extends its embrace to our everyday existence as well. It's in these fleeting moments of uncertainty that this story emerges as a guiding light, an embodiment of inspiration. While transforming the entire world might appear a Herculean feat, we can, at the very least, kindle transformation in the lives of those who cross our path.

A universal truth holds that procrastination often arises from the overwhelming weight of challenges. A powerful antidote involves breaking down these monumental tasks into digestible fragments, addressing them one by one – mirroring the boy's approach, each starfish a testament to his unwavering commitment. To that solitary starfish, such an act radiates ripples of transformation, underscoring the immense impact that even the smallest gestures can wield

FEARLESS THINKING… The Star Fish

1: What small contribution can you make to lighten your load

2. What small contribution can you make in your own friends network to lighten someone else load?

NOW TAKE ACTION:

In the exploration of oneness, we've uncovered a profound interconnectedness that shapes our lives and the universe itself. The concept of oneness, where everything is intertwined and interdependent, carries a powerful message that extends from the microcosms of our cells to the vast expanses of space. This realisation offers us a path to deeper understanding, harmony, and positive change in our lives and the world around us.

Embrace Oneness: Reflect on the idea of oneness and its implications in your daily life. Recognise that you are part of a larger whole, connected to everything and everyone. Embrace the sense of unity and interconnectedness in your thoughts and actions.

Create Your Invisible Counsellors: Follow Napoleon Hill's concept of "Invisible Counsellors." Choose historical figures, thinkers, or individuals you admire, and engage in imaginary conversations with them. Seek guidance, insights, and wisdom from your chosen mentors.

Spread Positivity: Act as a source of positive energy in your community. Radiate love, joy, and unity in your interactions with others. Be a beacon of light that inspires those around you to embrace oneness and create a harmonious environment.

Nature Immersion: Spend time in nature to experience the oneness of the natural world. Engage in activities like gardening, yoga, or simply taking a walk to connect with the Earth's energy and strengthen your sense of interconnectedness.

Challenge Fear: Confront fear and negative thoughts that hinder your sense of oneness. When fear arises, acknowledge it, process it, and let it go. Replace fear with positive affirmations and focus on the interconnectedness that surrounds you.

Contribute to Unity: Extend the idea of oneness to your professional life. Align with your organisation's vision, values, and goals, fostering unity and collaboration. Make conscious efforts to work together for shared success.

In the tapestry of existence, each thread is woven into the fabric of oneness. By embodying this concept and taking action to live in harmony with it, you contribute to the evolution of a more connected, empathetic, and harmonious world. As Kabir, the 15th-century Indian saint, proclaimed, "The river and the waves are one surf: where is the difference between the river and the waves?" Let us all embrace our shared journey and weave a brighter future together.

Afterwards – The Promise of Our Time

In embracing these seven transformative steps, you're embarking on a journey to fearlessly shape a new, vibrant ecosystem while deepening your understanding of the rich tapestry of the universe. Within these steps lies the power to unlock your true potential, revealing that you are both the questions and the answers you seek. You are the very consciousness that illuminates your path, intricately woven into the fabric of life's diverse experiences. Your universe is a harmonious fusion of your unique encounters and your evolving self.

Fear, once acknowledged, paves the way for unbridled growth. Confront your fears, uncover what restrains you, and liberate your true essence. Nurture the seed of self-love and self-respect, fostering a garden of empowerment within. Embrace the dual journey of external learning and internal exploration, for in understanding yourself, you unveil the map to your purpose.

Joy is your compass, guiding you toward the activities that set your soul ablaze. Harness your innate gifts and talents to craft your North Star—a guiding light that propels you toward your aspirations. Surround yourself with a tribe that kindles your spirit, igniting your journey with shared passions and genuine connections.

As you tread the path of self-discovery, remember the art of lightening your load. A clear direction offers liberation, allowing you to travel unburdened towards your dreams. Yet, as you forge your own destiny, realise that your voyage is not solitary. You are part of a grand tapestry, a universal symphony that echoes the melody of existence.

In the symphony of life, you are both conductor and musician. The harmonious resonance of your actions, choices, and intentions reverberates through the interconnected web of existence. You are a single thread woven into the intricate fabric of the cosmos, a microcosm mirroring the macrocosm. Embrace this oneness, for in unity lies the power to shape not just your world, but the world around you.

As you step forward into this newfound understanding, remember that you are not just a traveller on this journey. You are the journey itself—an expedition of self-discovery, growth, and interconnectedness. Armed with these seven steps, you possess the tools to sculpt your destiny, paint your universe with vibrant hues, and dance to the rhythm of your own being.

The canvas of your life awaits your masterstroke. Paint boldly, for you are both the artist and the art.

Thank you for purchasing and reading my book. I am extremely greatful and hope you found value in reading it. Please consider sharing it with friends or family and leaving a review online. Your feedback and support are always appreciated, and allow me to continue doing what I love. Please go to my page on Amazon if you'd like to leave a review.

With heartfelt gratitude for sharing in this voyage,

Julia x

"Fleabag meets fairytale rollercoaster"
Charlie Brooks, actress

COLOURFUL CREATURES

JULIA LECKEY

Julia's Fiction Book: Colourful Creatures. Buy NOW from Amazon.

We each have five powerful life influencers; choose wisely, or face catastrophe.

"Profound - Fleabag meets Fairytale rollercoaster." Actress Charlie Brooks

Allow me to introduce Emily, also known as the Meerkat. She perceives those around her as unique creatures, a lens through which she navigates her bewildering and tumultuous world, along with its enigmatic inhabitants.

Endeavouring to forge ahead in life, Emily, a gifted and imaginative baker, establishes an extraordinary and enchanting business that prospers. However, she is soon drawn back into the web of manipulation and deceit she once sought desperately to escape. Her life collides uncontrollably as she grapples with suspicions, betrayal, love, and loss. Can she reclaim control of her destiny?

"Colourful Creatures" is a heart-warming, and uplifting narrative featuring an unconventional heroine whose inquisitiveness and cleverness beckons readers on an irresistible journey of self- discovery..

The sole path to survival lies in opening one's heart.

This extraordinarily vibrant novel comes to life through 130 meticulously crafted illustrations by 'Emma & Rose'. The audiobook, narrated by actress Charlie Brooks, adds an auditory dimension to this tale.

'Intriguing, original, and compelling.' Louise Court, Former Editorial Director, Hearst magazines, and Editor-in-chief of Cosmopolitan

'It takes no time at all to get invested in the characters of Colourful Creatures. I read this book in a day. Loved M from the start and was rooting for her, but all the characters are relatable because we all know someone like them. Enough plot twists to keep you hooked combined with the beautiful and clever illustrations - this is a very original novel.' Jacquie Beltrao, Journalist & Sky TV presenter.

'These Colourful Creatures have come alive and muscled their way into my brain - I've found myself thinking about them long after finishing the book. It's a tale of stressful times and worries that more and more of us will recognise - and some great home truths about the only way to find our inner calm.' Michelle Hather, Editor of Good Housekeeping

Acknowledgements

THANKYOU,

Firstly, to my husband, for the patience, love, and support it takes to put up with a woman, wife, and mother who wants so much to be fearless and driven: thank you, and I love you. Thank you to my boys, whom I drive bonkers with my endless talking about ideas, life, and work.

Then there are numerous fearless individuals whom I would like to express my gratitude to for the incredible adventures that have led me to this point. A special mention goes to Christina Alley, whose ideas, inspiration, and remarkable editing skills have played a crucial role. I am also immensely thankful to Michelle Hather for her dedication in reading and editing this work multiple times; your patience and effort are truly appreciated.

To the fearless women whom I interviewed and who graciously shared their stories, I am deeply grateful. Jacqueline Gold for believing in me and for giving me so much of her precious time. Antonia Belcher for her inspiring story, her tireless crusade for the trans movement, and for opening up to me in her interview. Ann Hemmings, who not only is a six-time world champion and Olympian, but also helped me get back on my feet when I was very low. In fact, she did more than that – she encouraged me to climb Mount Toubkal with her and her Olympian friends, pulling me out of self-pity and back into life again. Leanne Pero, for being such a shining light in the world; you are a leader of communities. Thank you to all the people whom I referenced in this book, who inspired me to get on with life—Louise Hay and Jim Rohn, you were legends in so many ways.

Last, and by no means least, a final thank you to my mum and dad, because what thank you would be complete without that, just as I would not be complete without them.

The Beginning

Let the conversation begin …

Follow me on Julia.leckey.com and my coaching company thinkingfearlessly.com and INSTA JuliaLeckeyAuthor

First published by Amazon KDP Front Cover Design by Marie Julie Trisson

Diagram here by Julia Leckey

ISBN: 978-9-69-379251-5

Thinking Fearlessly Ltd.

Printed in Great Britain
by Amazon

30413927R00167